Instant Optimizing Embedded Systems Using BusyBox

Learn to optimize embedded systems with BusyBox using practical, hands-on recipes

Wu Zhangjin

Cao Ziqiang

BIRMINGHAM - MUMBAI

Instant Optimizing Embedded Systems Using BusyBox

First published: November 2013

Production Reference: 1221113

Published by Packt Publishing Ltd.
Livery Place
35 Livery Street
Birmingham B3 2PB, UK.

ISBN 978-1-78328-985-1

www.packtpub.com

Credits

Authors
Wu Zhangjin

Cao Ziqiang

Reviewers
Kevin Boone

Gergely Gati

Jason Winnebeck

Acquisition Editor
Rubal Kaur

Commissioning Editors
Govindan K

Llewellyn Rozario

Technical Editors
Jinesh Kampani

Chandni Maishery

Copy Editor
Aditya Nair

Project Coordinator
Joel Goveya

Proofreader
Clyde Jenkins

Production Coordinators
Manu Joseph

Nilesh Bambardekar

Cover Work
Manu Joseph

Cover Image
Disha Haria

About the Authors

Wu Zhangjin studied Computer Science and Technology at Lanzhou University and obtained his Master's degree in Distributed and Embedded System in 2010. He is a Linux user and developer since 2004 and he co-founded the Open Source Community of Lanzhou University in 2006. He is an active open source contributor; he launched the Linux-Loongson/Community Project in 2009 and uploaded more than 100 patches to the Linux mainline. He reactivated the Tiny-Linux kernel project in 2011. He also developed some other open source projects, such as VnStatSVG and TP4CELL.

He worked for a Chinese Loongson CPU application company and a world-leading embedded system company and now works on Linux system optimization for a leading Chinese Android smartphone company.

Currently, his main focus includes real-time systems, Linux RAS, power saving, system fastboot, system-size optimization, and kernel debugging and tracing.

His private website is `http://tinylab.org`; it is mainly about embedded system research and development. The extra content related to this book project will also be discussed there.

Acknowledgments

We're constantly very appreciative of the help provided by open source developers and communities. During the course of this project, we used a lot of open source tools and got a lot of inspiration from answers to open questions. In no particular order, we'd like to express our gratitude to developers and communities of BusyBox, Android, Gnu Toolchain, Buildroot, Ubuntu, Linux Kernel, and other utilities from the embedded system world.

I wish to acknowledge my sincere appreciation for Nicholas McGuire and Qingguo Zhou, who were my university instructors; they brought me into the Linux world. I want to thank the team members from the Open Source Community of Lanzhou University, who worked with me to build an excellent Linux system study environment. Many thanks to our previous and current colleagues, who discussed embedded system issues together and strengthened my embedded system experience a lot.

I also want to thank Cao Ziqiang, the co-author of this book; without his professional work, it would have been impossible to complete this book on time. And many thanks to my girlfriend, Rogina Lee, for her patient support and encouragement in the writing process.

Finally, thanks to Packt Publishing, who invited us and gave us the opportunity to discuss embedded system optimization with developers from all over the world. A special thank you to the production team and the reviewers who worked with us during this project and gave us guidance and feedback.

Cao Ziqiang is a Linux fan since 2004, and has more than eight years of experience in using the Linux operating system. He has extensive experience in video programs and network programs in C/C++ under Linux and has also majored in Linux kernel and device-driver development. In recent years, he has paid more attention to system stability and robustness, and worked for a smartphone company that uses Android as their main software platform. He is good at analyzing and resolving problems at the development phase using Linux tools such as toolbox, BusyBox, and some other open source projects of the Linux community. As a participant, he tested and fixed bugs in the Google Samsung kernel community. This is his first book as a co-author. He sincerely believes in the sharing of experience, which he has done with this book, and he will not stop sharing.

I wish to thank Wu Zhangjin, who invited me to write this book as a co-writer, and also thank the editors of Packt Publishing, who gave us a lot of help on how the process would be compiled. I also wish to thank my girlfriend Krissy, who encouraged me to complete this book. I also wish to thank you for reading this book, and wish we could create a communication bridge between us. Thanks.

About the Reviewers

Kevin Boone has been developing software since the days 16 KB was a RAM upgrade. By the time a MB was starting to feel cramped, he'd worked on projects ranging in scale from heart pacemakers to oil platforms, and was teaching Software Engineering to other people. He earned his PhD at around the time an MB was an only modest memory size for a PDA. These days, Kevin spends most of his time working on server applications that struggle to fit into a GB; nevertheless, he maintains and contributes to a number of open source projects associated with embedded Linux and Android. On those rare occasions when he isn't slumped in front of a computer screen, Kevin enjoys playing the piano, outdoor sports, and being a dad.

Gergely Gati began programming in the mid-eighties on a Commodore 16. One of his first publicly available work was the CP4, a C=+4 emulator for Amiga, written in 90 percent assembly. Over the last ten years, he has gained experience in the embedded communication domain, especially in safety critical vehicle network systems. AUTOSAR is a CAR-OEM-supported open standard, which intended to be an answer to the increasing complexity of in-car networks. Gati played the main role in creating one of the first experimental AUTOSAR 2.1 applications. In his spare time, he works on mobile apps for Java and Android phones. His most popular app is Weather—`weather.midlets.eu`—which runs on basic Nokia phones to advanced smartphones.

Jason Winnebeck is a software developer with over 10 years of experience in Java technologies and embedded development and deployment on Linux-based platforms in military and commercial environments, as well as databases and RESTful web services. He holds a Master's degree in Computer Science from the Rochester Institute of Technology.

www.PacktPub.com

Support files, eBooks, discount offers and more

You might want to visit www.PacktPub.com for support files and downloads related to your book.

Did you know that Packt offers eBook versions of every book published, with PDF and ePub files available? You can upgrade to the eBook version at www.PacktPub.com and as a print book customer, you are entitled to a discount on the eBook copy. Get in touch with us at service@packtpub.com for more details.

At www.PacktPub.com, you can also read a collection of free technical articles, sign up for a range of free newsletters and receive exclusive discounts and offers on Packt books and eBooks.

http://PacktLib.PacktPub.com

Do you need instant solutions to your IT questions? PacktLib is Packt's online digital book library. Here, you can access, read and search across Packt's entire library of books.

Why Subscribe?

- ▶ Fully searchable across every book published by Packt
- ▶ Copy and paste, print and bookmark content
- ▶ On demand and accessible via web browser

Free Access for Packt account holders

If you have an account with Packt at www.PacktPub.com, you can use this to access PacktLib today and view nine entirely free books. Simply use your login credentials for immediate access.

Table of Contents

Preface

BusyBox is a free GPL-licensed toolbox aimed at the embedded world. It is a collection of the tiny versions of many common Unix utilities. It can be compiled into one single binary and it provides a fairly complete environment for any small or large embedded system.

It is specifically designed for resource-limited and requirement-diverse embedded systems. It was written for size optimization and is extremely modular and highly configurable for system customization. Besides, it allows us to easily integrate new applets and to build embedded systems with it as a system base.

It provides basic shell programming and running environment. With the help of system generation tools like Buildroot, other generic tools and development environments can be added into the target embedded system easily. The benefit of these environments is that the target system can be enhanced to meet diverse requirements.

Besides daily-use utilities, it provides lots of lightweight replacements for powerful optimization tools and allows us to optimize the embedded system in many aspects, such as size tailoring, system stability enhancements, power consumption saving, system boot speedup, and debugging and tracing.

Android, a free ASL-licensed smartphone platform, is designed, developed, and released by Google. Benefitting from its Apache Software License (ASL), lots of third-party companies joined and formed the Open Handset Alliance. Without worrying about using open Android with their own non-open proprietary software, they produced many famous Android smartphones and eventually expanded the popularity of Android.

Behind the success of Android is a huge development investment. A large number of powerful software components have been developed, including the Android Goldfish emulator, Goldfish Linux kernel, Bionic libc, Java VM Dalvik, SDK, and NDK. Besides a BusyBox-like toolbox is added, but it is licensed under ASL and tailor-made for Android, only include a few of utilities and some platform-specific applets.

For embedded system optimization, we have no reason not to choose the famous BusyBox and Android. BusyBox is used as the toolbox and Android as the target platform. Their combination makes the requirement clear, experiment practical, and demonstration easy to understand.

What this book covers

Configuring BusyBox (Simple) introduces from where to download BusyBox source code, how to configure it for a particular requirement using `defconfig`, `xxx_defconfig`, `oldconfig`, `allyesconfig/allnoconfig`, `menuconfig`, and `randconfig`.

Compiling BusyBox (Simple) reveals that BusyBox supports multiple architectures and explains how to compile them locally for an x86 host and how to cross-compile it for the ARM platform. Static linking and dynamic linking are also discussed here.

Installing BusyBox (Simple) will introduce how BusyBox applets are invoked in different methods and demonstrate how to install BusyBox on a local host at the compiling stage or at runtime. Besides, its elaborate use as a root filesystem is shown with the `chroot` command.

Creating a virtual Android device (Simple) will use an Android emulator to create a virtual Android device as our embedded experimental platform. A virtual Nexus 7 will be created and launched on an Android emulator. The debugging features, adb, and the serial port are also demonstrated.

Playing BusyBox on a virtual Android device (Intermediate) will show the usage of the cross-compiled BusyBox on the virtual Android device. It will hack the prebuilt Android ramdisk image and use the BusyBox `ash` shell instead of an Android toolbox `mksh` shell and start it as the default console. Besides, network services such as telnetd and httpd will be shown to provide a remote shell and launch a remote web service respectively.

Building BusyBox-based embedded system (Intermediate) talks in depth about an Android ramdisk image. It shows how to make a bootable BusyBox-based root filesystem and convert it to an Android ramdisk. To boot it on an Android Emulator, a new version of Linux kernel is required and compiled.

Adding new applets to a BusyBox-based embedded system (Intermediate) introduces methods to enhance the functionality of BusyBox-based embedded systems. It shows how to integrate new lightweight applets. Besides this, it also teaches how to build standalone tools (Bash) and build utilities (C programming environment) with the automatic system, Buildroot.

Tailoring the system size of an embedded (Android) system (Advanced) will show you how to optimize the size of an embedded system to reduce disk and memory footprint and reserve more free storage for end users. Tools such as size is demonstrated.

Reducing the power consumption of an embedded (Android) system (Advanced) will discuss the common methods used to reduce power cost and show the usage of a power cost measuring tool called PowerTOP. The tools on an Android system, such as `dumpsys alarm`, `dumpsys power`, and `/proc/wakelocks` or `/d/wakelocks` interfaces, are also introduced.

Speeding up the system boot of an embedded (Android) system (Advanced) talks about how to reduce the time cost from system power on to the display of the graphic UI using both common methods and the measuring tool, bootchart. Besides, the grabserial tool is recommended for measuring the time taken for bootloader and kernel booting.

Enhancing the system stability of an embedded (Android) system (Advanced) shows the common methods to enhance system stability; the test automation method with the shell environment provided by BusyBox is discussed in depth with an open source Linux Device Driver Test framework: OMAP DDT. Also, Android tools such as CTS and monkeyrunner are introduced.

Increasing the serviceability of an embedded (Android) system (Advanced) introduces the methods to restore the failure generation scene; they include system logging, system debugging, and tracing. The Linux Kernel built-in debugfs, sysfs, procfs and Ftrace are discussed. The BusyBox built-in `top`, `iostat`, and `devmems` are demonstrated. Android-specific tools such as `ram console`, `logger/logcat`, and `systrace` are also introduced.

What you need for this book

BusyBox is a free GPL-licensed open source software. It can be downloaded easily from its main site or other mirror sites. An Ubuntu host is preferred for performing experiments and it's even better with a real (rooted) Android device.

Who this book is for

This book is written specifically for embedded system developers and Android developers who wish to optimize system performance. The prerequisites are basic knowledge of Linux and Unix utilities. This book also helps new developers start with BusyBox and Android development.

Conventions

In this book, you will find a number of styles of text that distinguish between different kinds of information. Here are some examples of these styles, and an explanation of their meaning.

Code words in text, database table names, folder names, filenames, file extensions, pathnames, dummy URLs, user input, and Twitter handles are shown as follows: "In this recipe, we'll download BusyBox and configure it using `defconfig`, `xxx_defconfig`, `oldconfig`, `allyesconfig/allnoconfig`, `menuconfig`, and `randconfig`."

A block of code is set as follows:

```
# Start httpd service
httpd -h /data/www -p 8080
# Start telnetd service
telnetd -f /data/telnetd.issue -p 3333 -l /bin/ash
```

Any command-line input or output is written as follows:

```
$ adb forward tcp:3333 tcp:3333
$ adb forward tcp:8080 tcp:8080
```

New terms and **important words** are shown in bold. Words that you see on the screen, in menus or dialog boxes for example, appear in the text like this: "Start the AVD manager with android avd, choose the just created AVD and click on **Start**, choose **Scale display to real size** and click on **Launch** to start it.".

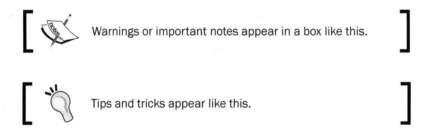

Warnings or important notes appear in a box like this.

Tips and tricks appear like this.

Reader feedback

Feedback from our readers is always welcome. Let us know what you think about this book—what you liked or may have disliked. Reader feedback is important for us to develop titles that you really get the most out of.

To send us general feedback, simply send an e-mail to feedback@packtpub.com, and mention the book title via the subject of your message.

If there is a topic that you have expertise in and you are interested in either writing or contributing to a book, see our author guide on www.packtpub.com/authors.

Customer support

Now that you are the proud owner of a Packt book, we have a number of things to help you to get the most from your purchase.

Downloading the example code

You can download the example code files for all Packt books you have purchased from your account at http://www.packtpub.com. If you purchased this book elsewhere, you can visit http://www.packtpub.com/support and register to have the files e-mailed directly to you.

Errata

Although we have taken every care to ensure the accuracy of our content, mistakes do happen. If you find a mistake in one of our books—maybe a mistake in the text or the code—we would be grateful if you would report this to us. By doing so, you can save other readers from frustration and help us improve subsequent versions of this book. If you find any errata, please report them by visiting http://www.packtpub.com/submit-errata, selecting your book, clicking on the **errata submission form** link, and entering the details of your errata. Once your errata are verified, your submission will be accepted and the errata will be uploaded on our website, or added to any list of existing errata, under the Errata section of that title. Any existing errata can be viewed by selecting your title from http://www.packtpub.com/support.

Piracy

Piracy of copyright material on the Internet is an ongoing problem across all media. At Packt, we take the protection of our copyright and licenses very seriously. If you come across any illegal copies of our works, in any form, on the Internet, please provide us with the location address or website name immediately so that we can pursue a remedy.

Please contact us at copyright@packtpub.com with a link to the suspected pirated material.

We appreciate your help in protecting our authors, and our ability to bring you valuable content.

Questions

You can contact us at questions@packtpub.com if you are having a problem with any aspect of the book, and we will do our best to address it.

Instant Optimizing Embedded System Using BusyBox

Welcome to *Instant Optimizing Embedded System Using BusyBox*.

BusyBox is a popular Unix toolbox; it integrates tiny versions of many common Unix utilities. It can be easily configured and compiled into a small, single-binary executable file. The built-in utilities are also known as BusyBox applets; they can be easily installed on an embedded system to add functionality or optimize performance. They can together also be used to build new embedded systems with extra device nodes, configuration files, and a Linux kernel.

This book will walk you through the configuration, compiling, and installation of the single-binary Unix toolbox, BusyBox. We'll show its basic usage on a desktop development system and the Android emulator, build a bootable embedded system from scratch and boot it on a virtual Android device, discuss how to meet diverse function requirements of BusyBox-based embedded systems, and explore how to utilize some powerful built-in applets to optimize different aspects of an embedded system.

Throughout this book, Ubuntu, as the most popular Linux distribution, will be used as our default desktop development system. Android, as the most popular embedded Linux system, will be used as our target embedded system. Android emulator, as the easy and cheap way to get a running Android device with root permission, will be used to build the Android experiment platform for demonstration.

Configuring BusyBox (Simple)

In this recipe, we'll download BusyBox and configure it using `defconfig`, `xxx_defconfig`, `oldconfig`, `allyesconfig/allnoconfig`, `menuconfig`, and `randconfig`.

Getting ready

BusyBox was designed for Linux in early 1996, originally as a Debian GNU/Linux installer and rescue system. With about 18 years of development, the latest 1.21.0 (at the time of this writing) release has more than 380 applets and about 100 projects claimed using it. The projects embrace Linux, Android, FreeBSD, and others.

It integrates a set of stripped-down Unix tools, including simple ones, such as `echo` and `ls`, as well as the larger ones, such as `grep`, `awk`, `find`, `mount`, and `modprobe` and other functional utilities; for example, `ifconfig`, `route`, `dmesg`, `tar`, `wget`, and even a tiny shell interpreter called `ash`.

It is modular, and can be customized to meet different requirements. To discuss and demonstrate its configuration system, first download its source code. It is maintained at `http://git.busybox.net/busybox/` and released with `.tar` packages at `http://busybox.net/downloads/`. If you want a stable release, download the `.tar` packages or clone the Git repository with the latest (but perhaps not stable) features. At the time of this writing, we used the stable version `busybox-1.21.0.tar.bz2`; download it and decompress it.

```
$ wget http://busybox.net/downloads/busybox-1.20.0.tar.bz2
$ tar jxvf busybox-1.20.0.tar.bz2
$ cd busybox-1.20.0/
```

To simplify the command-line output, all command-line prompts in the desktop development system is prefixed with the $ symbol; ones that need root permission will follow a `sudo` command.

Before configuring, make sure the `ncurses` library required by the graphic configurator is installed on the development system.

```
$ sudo apt-get install libncurses5-dev
```

Downloading the example code

You can download the example code files for all Packt books you have purchased from your account at `http://www.packtpub.com`. If you purchased this book elsewhere, you can visit `http://www.packtpub.com/support` and register to have the files e-mailed directly to you.

How to do it...

The friendliest way to configure BusyBox will be using `make menuconfig`. Issue the command to launch a graphic interface, configure the features, and exit to save them.

1. Issue the following command in a graphic configurator:

    ```
    $ make menuconfig
    ```

2. It starts the graphic interface.

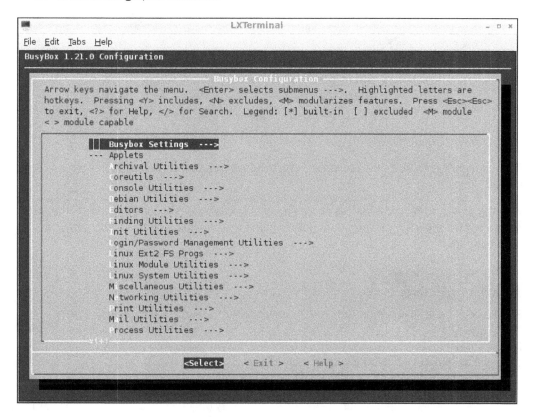

3. Configure the features with hotkeys. It allows us to enable, disable, exit, get help, and search with hotkeys. The primary hotkeys include:

    - **<Enter> selects submenus**
    - **<Y> includes**
    - **<N> excludes**
    - **<Space> Switch <Y> and <N>**

- ❏ **<Esc><Esc> to exit**
- ❏ **<?> for Help**
- ❏ **</> for Search**

4. Most configuration options are Boolean type. Use the `ash` shell applet as an example. Press *Enter* on the shell's submenu. Enable with *Y* and disable with *N*.

```
Shells  --->
[*] ash
```

5. Some configuration options are strings and may require input. Use the cross-compiler `arm-linux-gnueabi-gcc` (see the *Compiling Busybox* recipe) configuration as an example. Press *Enter* on `BusyBox Settings` and on `Build Options` and then press *Enter* on `(arm-linux-gnueabi-) Cross Compiler prefix`.

```
Busybox Settings  --->
        Build Options  --->
                (arm-linux-gnueabi-) Cross Compiler prefix
```

6. Save the configuration.

After configuring, Press *Esc + Esc* to exit, and the configuration will be saved to a file named `.config`.

With the previous configuration, we should be able to start the compiling process in the next recipe, but we still need to learn more details about the principle and the other methods of configuration.

How it works...

BusyBox can be flexibly customized; the main configurable features include `Busybox Settings` and `Applets`. The former allows us to configure build/compiling and installation features. The latter allows us to configure all of the built-in applets and their features. Both of them will be introduced in the following recipes.

To configure them in fine detail, the `Config.src` files (for example, `networking/Config.src`) provide configure options for the features, and every option should have a default setting.

Hotkeys are provided to enable, disable, or set the option; the option's value will be converted to symbols prefixed with `CONFIG_` and saved into the `.config` file, and meanwhile some C headers will be generated.

There's more...

Besides graphic configuration with `make menuconfig`, some other configuration techniques you might want to run with the BusyBox `make` tool include:

- ▸ `make config`: Similar to `make menuconfig`, this is a text-based interactive configurator. It does not contain the dependency of the `ncurses` library, and is not that friendly.

- ▸ `make oldconfig`: Resolve any unresolved symbols and regenerate C header files with the old configuration, `.config`; it is often executed after `make clean`. `make clean` allows us to delete temporary files created by an old configuration or building. It is often used to get a clean environment for a new configuration or building.

- ▸ `make xxx_defconfig`: Some old configurations, such as `.config` are renamed and saved to the `configs/` directory of the BusyBox source code. To re-use them, just run `make` with their names; for example:

    ```
    $ make android2_defconfig
    ```

- ▸ `make defconfig`: It uses the option's default setting and generates `.config` to the largest generic configuration. This is often used by a newcomer as the base of a new configuration. Based on this default configuration, disable the unnecessary features and reserve only the necessary features and get a minimal configuration eventually.

- ▸ `make allyesconfig/allnoconfig`: They don't use the default settings, but rather enable or disable the features and generate a `.config` file accordingly. Some options may still be disabled even with `allyesconfig`. If they conflict with the already enabled ones (for example, the `CONFIG_NOMMU` configure option is enabled by default), the other features, such as `ash`, will be disabled. `make allyesconfig` will generate the largest BusyBox binary. It should not be used to build a size-critical embedded system, but it may be a good configuration base for a rich-function system. `make allnoconfig` provides a clean configuration base. It may be good to get a clean configuration for a size-critical embedded system, but it requires a good understanding of the configuration options.

- ▸ `make randconfig`: It generates a configuration with random settings. We don't need it since our real requirement is often deterministic, but BusyBox developers may need it for building tests.

Compiling BusyBox (Simple)

After configuration, BusyBox can be compiled into a single binary for different architectures, with different compilers and with static or dynamic linking.

This recipe will compile BusyBox for our desktop development system as a quick demonstration, and meanwhile, build BusyBox for an ARM target platform as an embedded system case.

Getting ready

Before compiling a software, we must get a compiler and the corresponding libraries, a build host, and a target platform. The build host is the one running the compiler. The target platform is the one running the target binary built by the compiler from the software source code. Here, our desktop development system is our build host, and an ARM Android system will be used as our target platform.

To compile BusyBox on our desktop development system, we need a local compiler. Generally, most Linux operating systems ship with a working C compiler, and it's usually **GCC** (the **GNU Compiler Collection** is by far the most widely used C compiler on Linux, and can be downloaded from `http://gcc.gnu.org/`) and the corresponding **Glibc** (the **GNU C Library** by far is the most widely used C library on Linux and can be downloaded from `http://www.gnu.org/software/libc/`). If it isn't present, get one from our system's package manager for Ubuntu.

```
$ sudo apt-get install gcc g++ make build-essential
$ sudo apt-get install ia32-libs ia32-libs-multiarch
```

To compile BusyBox on our desktop development system for a different target architecture (for example, an ARM Android system), we need a cross-compiler.

ARM, as the most popular architecture on embedded system, is being used by more and more portable devices, such as the embedded Raspberry Pi board and the Android mobile phone or tablet, so we will concern ourselves with this alone.

The `gcc-arm-linux-gnueabi` cross-compiler can be installed directly on Ubuntu with the following command:

```
$ sudo apt-get install gcc-arm-linux-gnueabi
```

On other Linux distributions, Google's official NDK is a good choice if you want to share Android's Bionic C library, but since Bionic C library lacks of many POSIX C header files, and because we want to get the most out of BusyBox applets building, the prebuilt version of Linaro GCC with Glibc is preferable. We can download it from `http://www.linaro.org/downloads/`; for example, `http://releases.linaro.org/13.04/components/toolchain/binaries/gcc-linaro-aarch64-none-elf-4.7-2013.04-20130415_linux.tar.bz2`.

How to do it...

Let's compile BusyBox with the default configuration for our desktop development system as a quick demonstration of the compiling procedure and cross-compile it for the ARM platform as a real embedded system building example.

1. Compiling BusyBox for a desktop development system can be done as follows:

```
$ make defconfig
$ make
$ file busybox
busybox: ELF 64-bit LSB executable, x86-64, version 1 (SYSV),
dynamically linked (uses shared libs)...
$ ldd busybox
    linux-vdso.so.1 =>  (0x00007fff9edff000)
    libm.so.6 => /lib/x86_64-linux-gnu/libm.so.6
(0x00007f1cf2cb4000)
    libc.so.6 => /lib/x86_64-linux-gnu/libc.so.6
(0x00007f1cf28f5000)
    /lib64/ld-linux-x86-64.so.2 (0x00007f1cf2fcf000)
```

The previous lines of code compiled a binary for our x86-64 development
system (the output may differ if you are using a different development system)
and dynamically linked it with `libm.so` and `libc.so`.

2. To get a quick start, simply run the `echo` applet as an example.

```
$ ./busybox echo "Hello, Busybox."
Hello, Busybox.
```

3. To get help from BusyBox and its applets, we can append the `--help` command
as follows:

```
$ ./busybox --help
```

We see the following output:

```
BusyBox v1.21.0 (2013-09-06 01:24:09 CST) multicall binary.
BusyBox is copyrighted by many authors between 1998-2012. Licensed
under GPLv2. See source distribution for detailed copyright
notices.
Usage: busybox [function [arguments]...]
    or: busybox --list[-full]
    or: busybox --install [-s] [DIR]
    or: function [arguments]...
BusyBox is a multicall binary that combines many common Unix
utilities into a single executable file. Most people will create
a link to busybox for each function they wish to use and BusyBox
will act like whatever it was invoked as. Currently defined
functions:
[, [[, acpid, add-shell, addgroup, adduser, adjtimex, arp, arping,
ash, awk, base64, basename, beep, blkid, blockdev, bootchartd,
brctl, bunzip2, bzcat, bzip2, cal, cat, catv, chat, chattr,
```

chgrp, chmod, chown, chpasswd, chpst, chroot, chrt, chvt, cksum,
clear, cmp, comm, conspy, cp, cpio, crond, crontab, cryptpw,
cttyhack, cut, date, dc, dd, deallocvt, delgroup, deluser, depmod,
devmem, df, dhcprelay, diff, dirname, dmesg, dnsd, dnsdomainname,
dos2unix, du, dumpkmap, dumpleases, echo, ed, egrep, eject, env,
envdir, envuidgid, ether-wake, expand, expr, fakeidentd, false,
fbset, fbsplash, fdflush, fdformat, fdisk, fgconsole, fgrep, find,
findfs, flock, fold, free, freeramdisk, fsck, fsck.minix, fsync,
ftpd, ftpget, ftpput, fuser, getopt, getty, grep, groups, gunzip,
gzip, halt, hd, hdparm, head, hexdump, hostid, hostname, httpd,
hush, hwclock, id, ifconfig, ifdown, ifenslave, ifplugd, ifup,
inetd, init, insmod, install, ionice, iostat, ip, ipaddr, ipcalc,
ipcrm, ipcs, iplink, iproute, iprule, iptunnel, kbd_mode, kill,
killall, killall5, klogd, last, less, linux32, linux64, linuxrc,
ln, loadfont, loadkmap, logger, login, logname, logread, losetup,
lpd, lpq, lpr, ls, lsattr, lsmod, lsof, lspci, lsusb, lzcat,
lzma, lzop, lzopcat, makedevs, makemime, man, md5sum, mdev, mesg,
microcom, mkdir, mkdosfs, mke2fs, mkfifo, mkfs.ext2, mkfs.minix,
mkfs.vfat, mknod, mkpasswd, mkswap, mktemp, modinfo, modprobe,
more, mount, mountpoint, mpstat, mt, mv, nameif, nanddump,
nandwrite, nbd-client, nc, netstat, nice, nmeter, nohup, nslookup,
ntpd, od, openvt, passwd, patch, pgrep, pidof, ping, ping6, pipe_
progress, pivot_root, pkill, pmap, popmaildir, poweroff, powertop,
printenv, printf, ps, pscan, pstree, pwd, pwdx, raidautorun,
rdate, rdev, readahead, readlink, readprofile, realpath, reboot,
reformime, remove-shell, renice, reset, resize, rev, rm, rmdir,
rmmod, route, rpm, rpm2cpio, rtcwake, run-parts, runlevel,
runsv, runsvdir, rx, script, scriptreplay, sed, sendmail, seq,
setarch, setconsole, setfont, setkeycodes, setlogcons, setserial,
setsid, setuidgid, sh, sha1sum, sha256sum, sha3sum, sha512sum,
showkey, slattach, sleep, smemcap, softlimit, sort, split,
start-stop-daemon, stat, strings, stty, su, sulogin, sum, sv,
svlogd, swapoff, swapon, switch_root, sync, sysctl, syslogd,
tac, tail, tar, tcpsvd, tee, telnet, telnetd, test, tftp, tftpd,
time, timeout, top, touch, tr, traceroute, traceroute6, true,
tty, ttysize, tunctl, ubiattach, ubidetach, ubimkvol, ubirmvol,
ubirsvol, ubiupdatevol, udhcpc, udhcpd, udpsvd, umount, uname,
unexpand, uniq, unix2dos, unlzma, unlzop, unxz, unzip, uptime,
users, usleep, uudecode, uuencode, vconfig, vi, vlock, volname,
wall, watch, watchdog, wc, wget, which, who, whoami, whois, xargs,
xz,xzcat, yes, zcat, zcip.

Also we can use the echo command as follows:

```
$ ./busybox echo --help

BusyBox v1.21.0 (2013-10-16 01:24:09 CST) multi-call binary.

Usage: echo [-neE] [ARG]...
```

```
Print the specified ARGs to stdout

    -n  Suppress trailing newline
    -e  Interpret backslash escapes (i.e., \t=tab)
    -E  Don't interpret backslash escapes (default)
```

4. Now cross-compile it for the ARM platform. To compile it for the ARM platform, the cross-compiler `arm-linux-gnueabi-gcc` should be configured with `make menuconfig`, as we demonstrated in the previous recipe. After configuration, we can simply compile it as follows:

    ```
    $ make
    ```

5. Then a BusyBox binary is compiled for ARM with dynamic linking as follows:

    ```
    $ file busybox
    busybox: ELF 32-bit LSB executable, ARM, version 1 (SYSV),
    dynamically linked (uses shared libs), stripped
    ```

6. The previous `ldd` command of our development system doesn't work for listing the shared libraries required by the BusyBox binary for ARM,. Another command should be used instead, `arm-linux-gnueabi-readelf`, as follows:

    ```
    $ arm-linux-gnueabi-readelf -d ./busybox | grep "Shared library:" \
        | cut -d'[' -f2 | tr -d ']'
    libm.so.6
    libc.so.6
    ld-linux.so.3
    ```

7. To get the full path, we should first use the library search path.

    ```
    $ arm-linux-gnueabi-ld --verbose | grep SEARCH \
        | tr ';' '\n' | cut -d'"' -f2 | tr -d '"'
    /lib/arm-linux-gnueabi
    /usr/lib/arm-linux-gnueabi
    /usr/arm-linux-gnueabi/lib
    ```

8. Then we find out that `/usr/arm-linux-gnueabi/lib` is the real search path in our platform and we get the full path of the libraries as follows:

    ```
    $ ls /usr/arm-linux-gnueabi/lib/{libm.so,libc.so,ld-
    linux.so.3}
    /usr/arm-linux-gnueabi/lib/ld-linux.so.3   /usr/arm-linux-
    gnueabi/lib/libc.so   /usr/arm-linux-gnueabi/lib/libm.so
    ```

Using BusyBox on an ARM platform needs an ARM device. This will be introduced in the *Creating a virtual Android device (Simple)* and *Playing BusyBox on a virtual Android device (Intermediate)* recipes.

How it works...

The configuration not only generates a `.config` file with enabled features, but also produces a C header file, `include/autoconf.h`, that enables or disables the features with C macros. Based on these macros, the compiler determines which C context should be built in the last binary.

There's more...

By default, the binary is dynamically linked. To avoid the installation of shared libraries, to reduce the whole system size, and to reduce the time cost of runtime linking, static linking is often used for embedded system compiling.

To enable static linking, configure BusyBox as follows:

```
Busybox Settings --->
    Build Options --->
        [*] Build BusyBox as a static binary (no shared libs)
```

We get the following error when using a new Glibc to compile BusyBox with static linking:

```
inetd.c:(.text.prepare_socket_fd+0x7e): undefined reference to
`bindresvport'
```

We need to disable `CONFIG_FEATURE_INETD_RPC`, as follows, to avoid it:

```
Networking Utilities  --->
    [*] inetd
        [ ]    Support RPC services
```

Then, recompile it as follows:

```
$ make
```

Because it is statically linked, the required libraries will be linked into the last BusyBox binary. To run it on the target system, you only need to install the BusyBox binary (no shared libraries need to be installed).

The installation of BusyBox will be discussed in next recipe and the *Creating a virtual Android device (Simple)* recipe.

Installing BusyBox (Simple)

This recipe will talk about the installation of the BusyBox binary on our desktop development system. Later on, a minimal filesystem will be built with BusyBox and demonstrated with `chroot`.

After creating a virtual Android device in the next recipe, we will learn how to install BusyBox on a real embedded platform.

Getting ready

Just as a Swiss Army knife has multiple blades, a single BusyBox executable can be used to invoke many applets. BusyBox applets can be invoked in a number of different ways, explained as follows:

- Pass the applet name as the first argument. We use the `echo` applet as an example.

```
$ ./busybox echo 'Hello, Busybox.'
Hello, Busybox.
```

- The `busybox` binary can be renamed with the applet's name as follows:

```
$ cp ./busybox du
$ ./du -sh busybox du
664.0K busybox
664.0K du
```

This method may be useful if only one single applet is configured and built into the `busybox` binary. This avoids the need to pass the argument mentioned in the first point and avoids the creation of the extra links required in the following point.

- Hard links or soft links (symbol links) with applet names can also invoke applets.

```
$ ln -s busybox wc
$ echo "Hello, Busybox." | ./wc -w
2
```

This also avoids the need to pass the argument in the previous point; if more than one applet is configured, it is more lightweight than renaming the `busybox` binary as the links cost less storage than a real hard copy.

The installation of BusyBox means creating soft links for all of its built-in applets.

How to do it...

Busybox can be installed at runtime or at the earlier compiling stage.

1. Installing BusyBox at runtime with the `--install` command:

    ❏ To install it separately, rather than overwriting the original system utilities, enter its compiling directory and create a directory to store its applets, as follows:

    ```
    $ cd ~/tools/busybox
    $ mkdir -p ~/busybox/bin
    ```

    ❏ Afterwards, install it with the `--install` option.

    ```
    $ ./busybox --install ~/busybox/bin
    ```

    ❏ Soft links will be created for all of the built-in applets, to execute the recent installed applets, set the `PATH` variable in the shell startup script, and load it for immediate use.

    ```
    $ echo "export PATH=~/busybox/bin:\$PATH" >> ~/.bashrc
    $ source ~/.bashrc
    ```

    This installation method is used if there is a need to use BusyBox applets on an existing embedded system; for example, if we want to use the lightweight BusyBox `httpd` command on an Android system to build a web service: we can simply take BusyBox on board an Android system and install it at runtime. See the *Playing BusyBox on a virtual Android device (Intermediate)* recipe for more details.

2. Installing BusyBox at the compiling stage with `make install`:

    ❏ We can also install it during the compiling stage. We just need to configure the target directory as follows:

    ```
    Busybox Settings   --->
        Installation Options ("make install" behavior)   --->
            (~/tools/busybox/ramdisk/) BusyBox installation prefix
    ```

    ❏ Then type in `make install` and all the applets will be installed in ~/tools/busybox/ramdisk/.

    ```
    $ ls ~/tools/busybox/ramdisk/
    bin   linuxrc   sbin   usr
    ```

This installation method is often used when we want to build a minimal embedded filesystem with BusyBox, because it creates the basic directory architecture for us automatically during the compiling stage. See the *Building BusyBox-based embedded system (Intermediate)* recipe for more information.

How it works...

With `--install`, hard links are created. To create soft links (symbolic links), the `-s` option should be appended. Soft links must be used if the target installation directory (for example, `/bin/` provided by the Android ramdisk filesystem) is not in the same device as the directory (for example, `/data/` provided by another filesystem of Android) storing the BusyBox binary; if they are not, we will get the following failure errors:

- `busybox: /bin/[: Invalid cross-device link`
- `busybox: /bin/[[: Invalid cross-device link`
- `busybox: /bin/acpid: Invalid cross-device link`
- `busybox: /bin/add-shell: Invalid cross-device link`

To use the `-s` option, it should be enabled with the following configuration:

```
Busybox Settings   --->
   General Configuration   --->
      [*] Support --install [-s] to install applet links at runtime
```

Apart from the `--install` option, the `make install` command will install the `bin/busybox` binary in the target directory specified by `CONFIG_PREFIX`, and it classifies the applets and puts them into different directories based on the applets' setting in `include/applets.src.h`; for example, the following line specifies that `ls` should be installed to `/bin`:

```
IF_LS(APPLET_NOEXEC(ls, ls, BB_DIR_BIN, BB_SUID_DROP, ls))
```

There's more...

To demonstrate quickly how to experiment with the previous filesystem, we use the `chroot` command, which allows us to switch to a new root filesystem. In the *Building BusyBox-based embedded system (Intermediate)* recipe, we'll talk about how to fulfill such filesystems and make it bootable on virtual Android devices.

If BusyBox is dynamically linked, the shared libraries should be installed manually.

Use the shared libraries for our desktop development environment listed by `ldd` in the *Configuring BusyBox* recipe as an example.

```
$ ldd busybox
    linux-vdso.so.1 =>   (0x00007fff9edff000)
    libm.so.6 => /lib/x86_64-linux-gnu/libm.so.6 (0x00007f1cf2cb4000)
    libc.so.6 => /lib/x86_64-linux-gnu/libc.so.6 (0x00007f1cf28f5000)
    /lib64/ld-linux-x86-64.so.2 (0x00007f1cf2fcf000)
```

Except the virtual `linux-vdso.so.1` (or `linux-gate.so.1`), we should create the same directory architecture:

```
$ cd ~/tools/busybox/ramdisk
$ mkdir lib lib64
$ mkdir lib/x86_64-linux-gnu/
```

The directory architecture looks as follows:

```
lib
└── x86_64-linux-gnu
    ├── ld-2.15.so
    ├── libc-2.15.so
    ├── libc.so.6 -> libc-2.15.so
    ├── libm-2.15.so
    └── libm.so.6 -> libm-2.15.so
lib64
└── ld-linux-x86-64.so.2 -> /lib/x86_64-linux-gnu/ld-2.15.so
```

Then, copy libraries under `/lib` and `/lib64` of our desktop development environment to the directories under `~/tools/busybox/ramdisk` and create the corresponding soft links as follows:

```
$ cp /lib/x86_64-linux-gnu/libc-2.15.so lib/x86_64-linux-gnu/
$ cp /lib/x86_64-linux-gnu/libm-2.15.so lib/x86_64-linux-gnu/
```

```
$ cp /lib/x86_64-linux-gnu/ld-2.15.so lib/x86_64-linux-gnu/
$ ln -s lib/x86_64-linux-gnu/ld-2.15.so lib64/ld-linux-x86-64.so.2
$ cd lib/x86_64-linux-gnu/
$ ln -s libc-2.15.so libc.so.6
$ ln -s libm-2.15.so libm.so.6
```

After the installation of the shared libraries, we can start the BusyBox `ash` shell in a new root filesystem with `chroot`. `chroot` needs root permission with `sudo`.

```
$ sudo SHELL=/bin/ash chroot ~/tools/busybox/ramdisk/
```

The `SHELL` environment variable specifies the default shell interpreter for `chroot`; in our example, we use BusyBox `ash`.

With `chroot`, we are able to emulate the target embedded scene.

The installation of the shared libraries for ARM BusyBox is similar, so we will not give an example here. If BusyBox is statically linked, no need to install the extra libraries; we can simply install them and use `chroot` to perform the experiment.

Creating a virtual Android device (Simple)

We have already discussed the configuration, compiling, and installation of BusyBox; it's time to talk about its usage on embedded platforms, and then for system optimization.

Android is the most popular embedded Linux system, and our book uses it as the experiment platform. To simplify building the experiment environment, the open source and free Android emulator is used instead of the real Android devices throughout the whole book. As a prerequisite, a virtual Android device will be created in this recipe.

Compare to real Android devices, such as the Raspberry Pi board or an Android smartphone or tablet, the virtual Android device created by Android emulator is cheaper. Android emulator is free to download and it is already *rooted* (with root permission for using without any limitation). Of course, because it is software emulated, it may be slower (if your development system has a low-end hardware configuration).

If you want to perform the following experiments on a real Android device, please make sure the device is rooted; otherwise, some exercises may fail due to permission limitations. The rooting method is out of the scope of this book; please contact your product maker for the same.

Getting ready

To create a virtual Android device, the Android emulator and the related Android SDK Manager should be installed first. **ADT** (**Android Development Tools**) provides these tools; we can get it from `http://developer.android.com/sdk/index.html`.

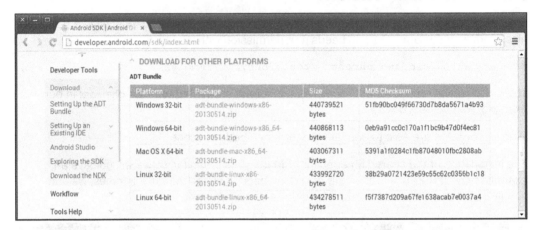

Download and use `adt-bundle-linux-x86_64-20130514.zip` for our x86-64 desktop development system. For other architectures, please download the proper version.

```
$ wget http://dl.google.com/android/adt/adt-bundle-linux-x86_64-
20130522.zip
```

```
$ sudo unzip adt-bundle-linux-x86_64-20130514.zip -d /usr/local/
```

```
$ sudo mv /usr/local/adt-bundle-linux-x86_64-20130514 /usr/local/adt-
bundle-linux
```

The tools required are installed at `/usr/local/adt-bundle-linux/sdk/`. Set the PATH variable in the shell startup script as before to set them permanently, so that they are easy to use:

```
$ echo "export SDK_ROOT=/usr/local/adt-bundle-linux/sdk/" >>
~/.bashrc
```

```
$ echo "export PATH=\$SDK_ROOT/tools/:\$PATH" >> ~/.bashrc
```

```
$ echo "export PATH=\$SDK_ROOT/platform-tools/:\$PATH" >> ~/.bashrc
```

```
$ source ~/.bashrc
```

With these settings, the tools like android, emulator, and adb are installed.

How to do it...

We use a virtual Nexus 7 device as our emulated experiment platform; its CPU is ARM with armeabi-v7a **ABI (Application Binary Interface)**, and runs Android 4.2 with **API (Application Program Interface)** level 17.

1. Create a virtual Android device with Android AVD Manager. Android allows us to quickly create an **AVD (Android Virtual Device)**. Let's create one named `busybox-avd`; first, launch the AVD manager interface with the following command:

   ```
   $ android avd
   ```

2. Click on the **New** button; start the configure interface and name it `busybox-avd`; choose Nexus 7 as the device name, and configure it as follows:

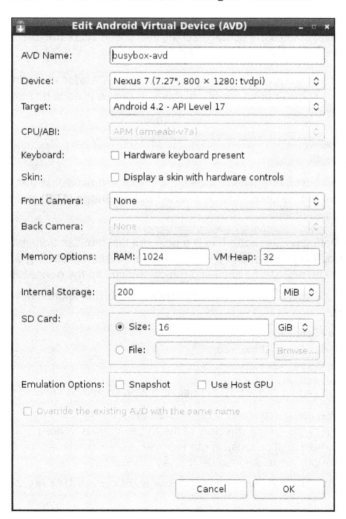

3. Click **OK** to finish creation.

4. Launch the virtual Android device with emulator.

   Start the AVD manager using `android avd`; choose the just created AVD and click on **Start**; choose **Scale display to real size**, and click on **Launch** to start it. After a while, the typical Android UI will be displayed.

5. It can also be started with the following command line:

```
$ emulator @busybox-avd -scale auto
```

`-scale auto` lets the emulator scale the windows to the real size of the virtual device.

How it works...

Google Android emulator, being based on QEMU, is an open source and free Bare Metal emulator. That is, it simulates the actual machine instruction set of the target system. This makes for a very accurate simulation, but it may be slow.

In reality, emulator is a wrapper and enhancement of QEMU. It adds the Goldfish platform emulation and adds some Android-specific features. It can be used to do most of the Android system development.

There's more...

Just as the real Android smartphone or tablet, the virtual Android device just created supplies with some development features, such as **Android Debug Bridge** (**ADB)** and the virtual serial-port-based shell environment.

- ▶ Android Debug Bridge (adb): This is a powerful tool that can transmit files between the development system and the target Android system (including our virtual Android device); it can also start a shell and run commands on the device and so forth.

  Use the `adb devices` command to check if the virtual Android device is connected, as follows:

```
$ adb devices
List of devices attached
emulator-5554   device
```

  The system setting of the USB debugging option should be enabled for this feature.

  We can also use it to transfer files; for example, download a prebuilt BusyBox for ARM and push it to the `/data` directory of the target Android device (`/data` stores the data of Android applications). In our example, we will download the one suffixed with `armv7l` for our virtual Android device `ABI: armeabi-v7a`.

```
$ wget http://busybox.net/downloads/binaries/latest/busybox-armv7l
```

```
$ adb push busybox-armv71 /data/busybox
```

Log in to Android from our development system, and experiment with our BusyBox on the Android device.

```
$ adb shell
root@android:/ # chmod 755 /data/busybox
root@android:/ # /data/busybox echo "Hello, Android."
Hello, Android.
```

The previous command lines log in to the Android shell with adb. Use the chmod command to make sure /data/busybox is executable. Finally, run the echo applet of BusyBox on Android.

adb also supports multiple devices; if many AVDs are connected together, the AVD can be specified via the serial number with the -s command, for example:

```
$ adb -s emulator-5554 shell
```

▸ Serial port debugging: To interact with the target system at the early development stage or to verify the low-level Linux drivers, we need another debugging tool, Serial port. This should be your first choice for debugging a just-launched embedded device or the last resort for tracking system statuses when the system is highly unstable.

The Android emulator supports the virtual serial port; to start AVD with the virtual serial port and Linux kernel log output, append the -shell -show-kernel command:

```
$ emulator @busybox-avd -scale auto -shell -show-kernel
shell@android:/ echo $SHELL
/system/bin/sh
shell@android:/
```

Note that the virtual serial port and Linux kernel log output belong to the Android system running on the Android emulator, not our development system.

The previous -shell command starts a console with a serial port, and -show-kernel enables Linux kernel log output. As we can see, a console is linked with the virtual serial port, and the default shell is /system/bin/sh.

If you only want to perform Linux kernel hacking, the -no-window command can be added to disable the graphic UI as follows:

```
$ emulator @busybox-avd -no-window -show-kernel -shell
```

Playing BusyBox on a virtual Android device (Intermediate)

This recipe uses a virtual Android device as the target platform that we just created to show the usage of BusyBox applets on an embedded platform. It will replace the Android toolbox `mksh` shell-based console with the more powerful BusyBox `ash` shell-based console. It starts a remote shell and a web service on it with BusyBox `telnetd` and `httpd` respectively.

The console based on BusyBox `ash` gives a more powerful shell environment. Not only can the applets be run on this console, but new shell scripts can also be written in such a shell environment.

The remote shell is useful for remote development and maintenance, and the web service is helpful for system monitoring. Both of them have common use cases in an embedded system.

Getting ready

At this stage, we aren't constructing a full bootable filesystem from scratch, but only using the BusyBox applets. So, for simplicity and ease of testing, we will install our compiled BusyBox binary and scripts into an existing Android `ramdisk` image.

At first, get a copy of the existing `ramdisk.img`; its path can be found at `~/.android/avd/busybox-avd.avd/hardware-qemu.ini`; for example, `adt-bundle-linux-x86_64/sdk/system-images/android-17/armeabi-v7a/ramdisk.img`.

How to do it...

Three examples will be shown in this section to demonstrate the usage of the BusyBox applets on a virtual Android device.

1. Replace the console based on Android mksh with the BusyBox ash console.

    Since the Android toolbox `mksh` shell is too lightweight, and the Android toolbox (the BusyBox-like toolset software) itself only provides a few of the applets, here it only shows us how to replace it with BusyBox `ash`. Start `ash` as the default console, and eventually build a more powerful shell environment.

    At first, decompress the original ramdisk image with the following steps:

    ```
    $ mv ramdisk.img ramdisk.img.gz
    $ gunzip ramdisk.img.gz
    $ mkdir ramdisk/ && cd ramdisk/
    $ cpio -i -F ../ramdisk.img
    ```

    Second, get a prebuilt BusyBox binary, `busybox-armv7l`, and put it into `ramdisk/`.

```
$ wget http://busybox.net/downloads/binaries/latest/busybox-
armv7l
$ cp busybox-armv7l ramdisk/
```

Third, to install BusyBox at runtime, let's prepare a script and name it `busybox-console.sh`, and add it into `ramdisk/`.

```
#!/system/bin/sh
# busybox-console.sh -- Install busybox to /bin and start /bin/ash


# remount root file system for read and write
mount -o remount,rw /
mkdir /bin
chmod 0777 /bin/
chmod 0777 /busybox-armv7l
/busybox-armv7l --install -s /bin


export SHELL=/bin/ash
/bin/ash
```

It remounts the root filesystem to be readable and writable and allows us to install BusyBox with `--install` to `/bin` at runtime; lastly, it starts `/bin/ash`.

```
$ cp busybox-console.sh ramdisk/
```

Then start a service in `init.rc` to launch the previous script. Add a `chmod` command to make sure the previous script is executable.

```
$ cd ramdisk/
$ sed -i '/loglevel/a \\n    chmod 0777 /busybox-console.sh'
init.rc
```

Let the BusyBox applets be executed directly without the full path.

Append the installation directory of the BusyBox applet, `/bin`, to the default PATH environment.

```
$ sed -i -e "s#export PATH #export PATH /bin:#g" init.rc
```

Replace the original console service with our console service that is based on `ash`.

```
$ sed -i -e "s#service console.*#service console
/bin/busybox.sh#g" init.rc
```

Now back up the old ramdisk and recompress a new one.

```
$ mv ramdisk.img ramdisk-backup.img
```

```
$ cd ramdisk/
$ find . | cpio -H newc -o | gzip -9 > ../ramdisk.img
```

Lastly, run the emulator to start with our new ramdisk and with the BusyBox `ash` console.

```
$ emulator @busybox-emulator -ramdisk ./ramdisk.img -shell -
show-kernel
/ # echo $SHELL
/bin/ash
/ # ls /bin
[                      fold              mke2fs              setsid
(truncated to fit in the text)
/ # which ls
/bin/ls
```

This code only lists a part of the applets installed. As we can see, the shell becomes `/bin/ash`. The applets are installed under `/bin` and the `ls` command is not the one provided by Android toolbox (`/system/bin/ls`) but the one (`/bin/ls`) installed by BusyBox. This indicates that we have successfully changed the console service to our own.

The writing of new shell scripts under this shell environment based on `ash` will be introduced in the *Enhancing system stability of an embedded (Android) system* recipe.

2. Start a remote shell with BusyBox `telnetd`:

    A real embedded system may have no serial port and adb and no local cable connected, but a network connection with Wi-Fi or 3G; accessing such systems may need a remote shell. As a lot of remote shells exist, such as SSH and Telnet, and since BusyBox doesn't provide an SSH daemon but `telnetd`, we use `telnetd` as an example here.

    Firstly, start the service on an emulator from a virtual serial port.

    ```
    / # echo "Hello, telnetd" > /data/telnetd.issue
    / # telnetd -f /data/telnetd.issue -p 3333
    / # ps | grep telnetd | grep -v grep
       731 0      0:00 telnetd -f /data/telnetd.issue -p 3333
    ```

    Second, build an emulated network connection. Android emulator does not provide a standalone full emulated network stack but a port-redirection-based network stack. In order to use the network service, the `adb forward` command should be used to enable the port redirection feature.

    Say you want to access the `telnetd` service seen previously. The remote tcp:3333 of the emulator must be redirected to a port of our desktop development system (for example, tcp:3333) by running the following command:

```
$ adb forward tcp:3333 tcp:3333
```

Third, log in to the telnet service and issue the following command on the development system:

```
$ telnet localhost 3333
Hello, telnetd
localhost login:
```

It means it really logs in and gets a prompt, Hello, telnetd. However, without a user account and the password, we cannot log in. To avoid setting up a username and password, we can simply let telnetd spawn /bin/ash rather than /bin/login, then no login progress will be required. Let's start telnetd on the emulator as follows:

```
/ # telnetd -p 3333 -f /data/telnetd.issue -l /bin/ash
```

Log in to the shell directly and experiment with our Android device remotely.

3. Start a web server with httpd:

Firstly, start httpd at /data/www, and create a simple HTML page on the target platform from a virtual serial port as follows:

```
/ # mkdir /data/www
/ # httpd -h /data/www -p 8080
/ # cat > /data/www/index.html
<!doctype html><html><head><title>BusyBox</title></
head><body><h1>Hello, Busybox Http Server Works.</h1></body></
html>
```

Second, just like telnetd, make a port redirection from the emulator to the development system.

```
# adb forward tcp:8080 tcp:8080
```

Lastly, let's access the httpd service with any modern web browser on our development system. Here we use the Chromium browser as an example:

How it works...

BusyBox applets cover the standard coreutils, console tools, e2fsprogs, procps, SELinux, editors, modutils, debianutils, login-utils, networking, sysklogd, util-linux, findutils, mailutils, printutils, and even a tiny shell interpreter. This recipe shows how to install some of them at runtime on an existing Android system and demonstrates the working of these three applets: `ash`, `telnetd`, and `httpd`.

To add more function for an embedded system, the other applets may also need to be configured via the configuration utility and used based on their full usage information with the `--help` command.

There's more...

In order to start the previously mentioned service during boot, we can add `httpd` and `telnetd` in the previous `/busybox-console.sh` script.

```
# Start httpd service
httpd -h /data/www -p 8080
# Start telnetd service
telnetd -f /data/telnetd.issue -p 3333 -l /bin/ash
```

To access them, we must also forward the remote ports to the development system as follows:

```
$ adb forward tcp:3333 tcp:3333
$ adb forward tcp:8080 tcp:8080
```

Building BusyBox-based embedded systems (Intermediate)

BusyBox can be used as a toolbox on existing systems, and it is also often used to build a bootable embedded system.

Let's build a standalone system with BusyBox from scratch and launch it on a virtual Android device with an Android emulator.

Getting ready

This recipe will use BusyBox to build our own filesystem and compress it to a `gzipped cpio` package, just like `ramdisk.img`, which we used in the previous recipe.

To boot such a new system, a new Linux kernel image should be compiled from Google Android-specific Linux kernel source code. Clone the source code for preparation.

```
$ cd ~/tools/busybox/
$ git clone https://android.googlesource.com/kernel/goldfish.git
```

The source code is specifically designed for Android goldfish hardware; the Android emulator won't run on other hardware.

To cross-compile an Android Linux kernel, the cross-compiler `arm-linux-gnueabi-gcc` should have been installed when going through the *Compiling BusyBox* recipe.

How to do it...

Based on the *Installing BusyBox* recipe, let's build our own filesystem: `ramdisk.img` with BusyBox from scratch, cross-compile our own Linux kernel image, and then boot them on the Android emulator:

1. Build a minimal Linux filesystem with BusyBox. To build a minimal bootable filesystem, the standard Linux filesystem directory architecture should be prepared at first.

    Apart from the /bin, /sbin, and /usr directories that are created by default, the /dev, /proc, /sys, and /etc directories must be created manually:

    ```
    $ cd ~/tools/busybox/ramdisk/
    $ mkdir dev sys etc proc
    ```

    /etc contains the configuration files for the Linux system. It includes two important files: inittab and fstab. inittab can be used by init to determine which programs should be run and fstab describes the filesystems mounting parameters. The init process is the first process invoked by the Linux kernel after the kernel finishes its initialization (to learn more about the generic boot sequence of a Linux system, read the manual page of the boot process by running the man boot command):

    ```
    $ cat > ./etc/inittab
    ::sysinit:/etc/init.d/rcS
    ttyS2::askfirst:/bin/sh
    ::restart:/sbin/init

    $ cat > ./etc/fstab
    proc /proc proc defaults 0 0
    sysfs /sys sysfs defaults 0 0

    $ mkdir ./etc/init.d
    $ cat > ./etc/init.d/rcS
    ```

```
#!/bin/sh
mount -a
echo /sbin/mdev > /proc/sys/kernel/hotplug
mdev -s
```

```
$ chmod 777 ./etc/init.d/rcS
$ ln -s ./sbin/init init
```

With the previous setting, during the booting of our Linux system, the init process parses our inittab file and runs /etc/init.d/rcS as the first action. It mounts all filesystems specified in fstab, and starts the minimal mdev device management tool (like the more famous tool, udev) to create all device nodes exported by low-level drivers under /dev for late operations. It also creates a console with /bin/sh, and attaches it at ttyS2. Since /sbin/init is the first user process, the /etc/inittab also let it respawn for system availability.

Lastly, the console based on /bin/sh is provided as the basic shell environment for the user interaction.

2. Package the filesystem into an image and name it ramdisk.img.

    Now, let's compress it with the following command:

    ```
    $ cd ramdisk/
    $ find . | cpio -H newc -o | gzip -9 > ../ramdisk.img
    ```

3. Cross-compile a new Android Linux kernel.

    To start our own ramdisk, since it doesn't work with the prebuilt kernel image (zImage) in Android ADT (Android Development Toolkit), we should build our own Linux kernel image from the Android Linux kernel source code. Go to the just downloaded goldfish/ directory and compile it as follows:

    ```
    $ cd ~/tools/busybox/goldfish/
    $ git checkout android-goldfish-3.4
    $ make goldfish_armv7_defconfig
    $ export CROSS_COMPILE=arm-linux-gnueabi-
    $ make zImage
    $ cp arch/arm/boot/zImage ~/tools/busybox/
    ```

4. Run our new embedded system on a virtual Android device.

    Now, start our own kernel image with the just-built minimal filesystem as follows:

    ```
    $ emulator @busybox-avd -shell -show-kernel -no-window \
    -kernel ./zImage -ramdisk ./ramdisk.img
    ```

```
Uncompressing Linux... done, booting the kernel.
...

Please press Enter to activate this console.
```

According to this message, we can press *Enter* to activate the console terminal and execute the commands that we want to run.

How it works...

The `ramdisk.img` is an archive of format `gzipped cpio`, which is extracted as the default root filesystem when the kernel boots up. It generally contains a file named `init`, which will run after the kernel boots up. This `init` command parses the initialization configuration, `/etc/inittab`, and eventually starts the console based on the `ash` shell, and provides the applets' running environment.

There's more...

In real embedded development with the minimal filesystem built with BusyBox and their built-in applets, we are able to verify the function and robustness of their device drivers through their exported `/dev`, `/sys`, and `/proc` interfaces.

With the help of the `ash` applet, shell scripts can be written to perform test automation to enhance the stability of an embedded system. With the help of the built-in PowerTop, bootchartd, top, iostat, devmem, and some other external utilities, the other aspects of an embedded system can be optimized to provide better user experience. The test automation and system optimization will be discussed in the coming recipes.

Adding new applets to a BusyBox-based embedded system (Intermediate)

If BusyBox built-in applets are not enough for our embedded requirement, new tools should be added.

This recipe shows three methods to integrate new utilities to a BusyBox-based embedded system.

Getting ready

In order to extend a fork of BusyBox by adding functionality from an existing utility, just compile and install the new utility as a separate binary, which will be explained later. But to distribute one binary exactly to our embedded system and get a smaller-sized system, integrating new applets into BusyBox is a direct method.

To do so, use the small `sstrip` program as an example. `sstrip` is a small utility that removes the contents at the end of an ELF file that are not part of the program's memory image. ELF (`http://en.wikipedia.org/wiki/Executable_and_Linkable_Format`) is the common standard file format for Linux executables.

Download it with SVN or download it from this link: `https://dev.openwrt.org/browser/trunk/tools/sstrip/src/sstrip.c`. In our example, use `svn` to check it out.

```
$ cd ~/tools/
$ svn co svn://dev.openwrt.org/openwrt/trunk/tools/sstrip
```

How to do it...

To add the `sstrip` program into BusyBox, follow these steps:

1. Add the original tool to the BusyBox source code:

   The new applet should be added to a suitable directory of BusyBox. In our example, `sstrip` is a `misc` utility so we add it to `miscutils/`.

   ```
   $ cd ~/tools/busybox/
   $ cp ../sstrip/src/sstrip.c miscutils/sstrip.c
   ```

2. Provide an applet-specific main entry, `sstrip_main()`:

   The entry of a new applet should be named `applet_main()`. For `sstrip`, it should be `sstrip_main()`.

   ```
   $ sed -i -e "s/int main/int sstrip_main/g" miscutils/sstrip.c
   ```

3. Add usage information:

   Add the trivial and full usage macros into `miscutils/sstrip.c`.

   ```
   //usage:# define sstrip_trivial_usage
   //usage:# "sstrip FILE..."
   //usage:# define sstrip_full_usage "\n\n"
   //usage:# "sstrip discards all nonessential bytes from an
      executable.\n\n"
   //usage:# "Version 2.0-X Copyright (C) 2000,2001 Brian
      Raiter.\n"
   //usage:# "Cross-devel hacks Copyright (C) 2004 Manuel
      Novoa III.\n"
   //usage:# "This program is free software, licensed under
      the GNU\n"
   //usage:# "General Public License. There is absolutely no
      warranty.\n"
   ```

By default, the trivial usage is added to minimize the size of the compiled binary, but if you want verbose output with full usage information, the `CONFIG_FEATURE_VERBOSE_USAGE` option should be enabled.

4. Add configuration support:

   We add the configuration description at the end of `miscutils/Config.src`.

   ```
   config SSTRIP
       bool "sstrip"
       default n
       help
       sstrip is a small utility that removes the
       contents at the end of an ELF file that
       are not part of the program's memory image.
   ```

   This allows users to enable or disable the `sstrip` applet via the configuration utility.

5. Add compiling support:

   Add compiling support at the end of `miscutils/Kbuild.src`.

   ```
   lib-$(CONFIG_SSTRIP)        += sstrip.o
   ```

   This builds the `sstrip` binary in the last BusyBox binary when the `CONFIG_SSTRIP` configure option is enabled.

6. Add macros declaration about main entry, usage information, links, and the installation directory:

   Add the following line to `include/applets.src.h` to add the necessary macros.

   ```
   IF_SSTRIP(APPLET(sstrip, BB_DIR_USR_SBIN, BB_SUID_DROP))
   ```

   It lets BusyBox install `sstrip` to `/usr/bin` at the compiling stage with `make install`, and also exports the macros about the main entry, usage information, and links.

7. Use common header files:

   Later, replace all of its header files except `<elf.h>` with `libbb.h`.

8. Configure and compile it:

   To build `sstrip` in the BusyBox binary, enable it with `make menuconfig`:

   ```
       Miscellaneous Utilities   --->
           [*] sstrip
   ```

   The `docs/new-applet-HOWTO.txt` file provides more information about how to add a new applet, but part of it is out of date. Real examples may be better references; for example, `miscutils/chrt.c`.

How it works...

BusyBox is modular and highly configurable. As seen previously, a new applet can be easily integrated, except renaming the main entry. The configure, build, and header files are added or modified for configuration, compiling, and installation respectively.

Since the `main()` entry is used by the BusyBox binary itself, the other applets' entries should be renamed with their own names.

The change in `miscutils/Config.src` adds a configure symbol, `CONFIG_SSTRIP`, with respective help information.

The modification in `miscutils/Kbuild.src` allows `sstrip` to be compiled while the `CONFIG_SSTRIP` symbol is enabled.

The addition in `include/applets.src.h` declares the prototypes of the new applet, `sstrip`, and the respective usage, main entry, and links.

There's more...

Lightweight tools like `sstrip` can be simply integrated into the BusyBox package. But for getting more functional utilities for our embedded systems, such methods don't work. However, we do have two other methods.

- ▶ Build standalone tools:

    One method is to compile the existing tools independently and then add them into a BusyBox-based embedded system.

    As an example, we add a more powerful shell interpreter, Bash 4.2, into a BusyBox-based embedded system, and then download and compile it for ARM.

    ```
    $ sudo apt-get install bison autoconf
    $ cd ~/tools
    $ git clone git://git.savannah.gnu.org/bash.git
    $ cd bash
    $ git checkout -b bash-4.2 f281b8f4f
    $ ./configure -host=arm-linux-gnueabi --enable-static-link \
        --without-bash-malloc
    $ make
    ```

    Now the compiled Bash can be put into `ramdisk.img` and used instead of BusyBox `ash`. Note that Bash is really powerful for writing shell scripts, but does cost more storage. It should not be used for a size-critical embedded system but rather for testing.

▸ Automated building systems:

Another method is to use automated building system; such systems include Buildroot. Buildroot can automate the procedure we performed in the *Building BusyBox-based embedded system (Intermediate)* recipe. It facilitates the generation of a complete embedded Linux system. It not only includes a root filesystem and a kernel image, but also a cross-compilation toolchain and a bootloader image. The root filesystem integrates BusyBox and other powerful utilities, and even programming environments.

To build `ramdisk.img` automatically with Buildroot, create a configuration file, `android_emulator_ramdisk_defconfig`, first:

```
# architecture
BR2_arm=y
BR2_cortex_a8=y
BR2_EXTRA_GCC_CONFIG_OPTIONS="--with-fpu=vfpv3 --with-float=hard"
# BR2_SOFT_FLOAT is not set

# system
BR2_TARGET_GENERIC_HOSTNAME="android-emulator"

# development files, required by develop tools
BR2_DEPRECATED=y
BR2_HAVE_DEVFILES=y

# gcc
BR2_PACKAGE_GCC_TARGET=y

# package with cpio+gzip for init ramfs
BR2_TARGET_ROOTFS_CPIO=y
BR2_TARGET_ROOTFS_CPIO_GZIP=y
# BR2_TARGET_ROOTFS_TAR is not set

# bash shell
BR2_PACKAGE_BUSYBOX_SHOW_OTHERS=y
BR2_PACKAGE_BASH=y
```

This configuration file allows us to build a BusyBox-based embedded system in the `gzipped cpio` archive with GCC and Bash support for the ARM target with Cortex A8 CPU.

Now download, configure, and compile it as follows:

```
$ cd ~/tools

$ wget http://www.buildroot.org/downloads/buildroot-2013.05.tar.bz2
```

```
$ tar jxf buildroot-2013.05.tar.bz2
$ cp android_emulator_ramdisk_defconfig .config
$ make oldconfig
$ make
```

The default major number of `ttyS` device is not the same as the Android `ttyS` device.

```
$ adb shell cat /proc/devices | grep ttyS
253 ttyS
```

The default `tty` console is not `ttyS0`, but `ttyS2`. So, we need to fix them and repackage `ramdisk.img`.

```
$ sed -i -e '/ttyS\t/s#4\t#253\t#g'
system/device_table_dev.txt
$ sed -i -e "/ttyS0/ittyS2::respawn:/sbin/getty -L ttyS2
115200 vt100" output/target/etc/inittab
$ make
```

After compiling, a target ramdisk image, `output/images/rootfs.cpio.gz`, should be ready for the Android emulator.

```
$ cp output/images/rootfs.cpio.gz ramdisk.img
$ emulator @busybox-avd -ramdisk ./ramdisk.img \
-show-kernel - shell -no-window
...
Welcome to Buildroot
android-emulator login:
```

After booting, log in as a `root` user. We can use the native GCC compiler directly without any extra configuration. The `-no-window` option disables window output for this simple root filesystem, and it doesn't include window support.

If you want to avoid some of the pitfalls of cross-compilation and want to build C applications directly on the Android device as an exercise, a native C programming environment can be built for Android system by creating another configuration file, `android_emulator_defconfig`.

```
# architecture
BR2_arm=y
BR2_cortex_a8=y
BR2_EXTRA_GCC_CONFIG_OPTIONS="--with-fpu=vfpv3 --with-float=hard"
# BR2_SOFT_FLOAT is not set

# system
```

```
BR2_TARGET_GENERIC_HOSTNAME="android-emulator"

# development files, required by develop tools
BR2_DEPRECATED=y
BR2_HAVE_DEVFILES=y

# gcc
BR2_PACKAGE_GCC_TARGET=y

# don't compile busybox in
BR2_INIT_NONE=y
# BR2_PACKAGE_BUSYBOX is not set

# don't tar of the rootfs
# BR2_TARGET_ROOTFS_TAR is not set
```

This configuration file tells us to compile the native compiler, GCC, for our ARM target device without BusyBox support and without packaging the target root filesystem.

Now, configure and compile it as follows:

$ cp android_emulator_defconfig .config

$ make oldconfig

$ make

Then prepare a configuration, native-gcc.rc, for the setting of environment variables as follows:

```
# Compile and Using uClibc library based native gcc
compiler in Android system
export GCC_VER=4.7.3
export GCC_HOME=/data/gcc/
export GCC_NAME=arm-buildroot-linux-uclibcgnueabi
export GCC_LIB=$GCC_HOME/usr/lib/gcc/$GCC_NAME/$GCC_VER/
export GCC_LIBEXEC=$GCC_HOME/usr/libexec/gcc
/$GCC_NAME/$GCC_VER/
export PATH=$GCC_HOME/bin:$GCC_HOME/sbin:
$GCC_HOME/usr/bin:$GCC_HOME/usr/sbin:$PATH
export PATH=$GCC_HOME/usr/lib/ldscripts/:
$GCC_LIB:$GCC_LIBEXEC:$PATH
export LD_LIBRARY_PATH=$GCC_HOME/usr/lib:
$GCC_HOME/lib:$GCC_LIB:$GCC_LIBEXEC:$LD_LIBRARY_PATH
export LIBRARY_PATH=$LD_LIBRARY_PATH
export C_INCLUDE_PATH=$GCC_HOME/usr/include:
$GCC_LIBEXEC/include/:$GCC_LIBEXEC/include-fixed

[ ! -d /lib ] && mkdir /lib
```

```
ln -sf $GCC_HOME/lib/ld-uClibc.so.0 /lib/ld-uClibc.so.0
```

This file mainly configures the `PATH`, `LD_LIBRARY_PATH`, `LIBRARY_PATH`, and `C_LINCLUDE_PATH` environment variables to let GCC works as is.

At last, let's push the target directory and configuration to the Android system, and use the native GCC to compile a simple program as follows:

```
$ adb push output/target /data/gcc
$ adb push native-gcc.rc /data/
$ adb shell
root@android:/ # source /data/native-gcc.rc
root@android:/ # echo -e '#include <stdio.h>\nmain(void){
printf("Hello, Android\\n"); }' | gcc -xc -o t - && ./t
Hello, Android
```

In reality, with Bash (the popular shell-scripting environment) and with C (the popular native programming environment), we're able to re-use lots of existing shell scripts, C software, or write new ones for our BusyBox-based embedded system to enhance its functionality to a very flexible extent.

Tailoring the system size of an embedded (Android) system (Advanced)

We have now discussed the basic configuration, compiling, installation, and usage of BusyBox on virtual Android devices and demonstrated how to build a bootable embedded system with BusyBox from scratch and enhanced the system through integrating additional utilities, including lightweight applets, standalone tools, and even programming language environments. In short, the functionality implementation of a scalable embedded system with BusyBox has been discussed in depth in previous recipes.

This recipe onwards, we will learn how to enhance user experience—it's time to talk about system optimization. Size optimization will be discussed in this recipe.

Getting ready

For most embedded systems (particularly consumer electronics like smartphone systems), due to the limitation of product cost, size of the hardware model, and rich-function requirements, system image size should be limited to fit the size of the disk and memory and reserve more free storage for end users.

How to do it...

The software of an embedded Linux system mainly includes bootloader, kernel, ramdisk, system, and applications. Use the embedded filesystem we just built with BusyBox in the *Building BusyBox-based embedded system (Intermediate)* recipe as an example. To reduce its size, we should:

1. Demand determine features:

   Remove the functions that are not required by the target system by disabling those features, via the configuration utility.

   For example, use `defconfig` as a configuration base and enable the necessary features and disable the rest.

2. Share common features in libraries:

   When adding new features to BusyBox, try to use the library functionality already present in BusyBox and remove the code from the utility that duplicates that functionality.

   For example, for the `sstrip` program we just integrated, if some of its functions already exist in the common libraries of BusyBox, they should be removed.

3. Static linking versus dynamic linking:

   If possible, link BusyBox with a lightweight standard library such as uClibc (`http://www.uclibc.org/`; it is optimized for an embedded system and is smaller than Glibc), not Glibc.

   If extra tools are required and support dynamic linking to share the same library, don't link BusyBox statically. But if you only need BusyBox, link statically to avoid the need of a dynamic linker and loader.

4. Utilize compiler and linker support:

   Enable the `-Os` option of GCC by disabling the `CONFIG_DEBUG_PESSIMIZE` configuration option of BusyBox and enable `--gc-sections` using not Glibc (see the comments in `scripts/trylink`), and with a new enough `ld` tool.

5. Strip everything that is not required at runtime:

   Use `strip` to discard symbols from object files, and use `sstrip` to remove the section header table at the end of the executable.

   It should be noted that an executable file that has no section header table cannot be used with gdb or objdump for debugging. You can learn more from the comments of `sstrip.c`.

6. Compression is a technique with external perspective:

   Instead of optimizing the size of the filesystem, compressing the whole filesystem image with a suitable algorithm is a technique with external perspective. The algorithms include a general `gzip` or `lzma` format with higher compression rate, and LZO or LZ4 with lower compression rate but faster decompression speed.

   For example, the embedded filesystem we created in the *Building BusyBox-based embedded system (Intermediate)* recipe is packaged in cpio format and finally compressed with gzip.

   To use such algorithms, corresponding decompression support is required in bootloader, or else the Linux kernel for the filesystem will be unpacked into memory at boot time.

7. Measure before starting optimization:

   Find the objects consuming large storage by measuring the size of each object or executable file and then optimize them one by one. The tools include `ls -l`, `du`, `size`, and `nm -size`.

   For example, the `size` utility can be used to output the size of different segments of an executable as follows:

```
$ size busybox
    text    data     bss     dec     hex    filename
  824447    4154    9520  838121   cc9e9    busybox
```

How it works...

The main storage consumers of an embedded Linux system are executables. A standard Linux executable is in an ELF format. Besides an ELF header, a program header table, and a section header table, it consists of the text segment, data segment (initialized), and BSS segment (uninitialized).

To optimize size means to remove unnecessary executables or to reduce the size of the previously mentioned segments of the executables by sharing common functions or data, or even via sharing a single ELF header.

BusyBox is highly modular and configurable, and therefore allows to choose only the necessary applets based on the real system requirements. And as a single binary, all of the built-in applets share one ELF header and share all of the common functions. Besides those, compiler size optimization options like -Os and --gc-sections are also well supported.

Also, the last binary can be stripped with `strip` and `sstrip`, and the generated filesystem image can be compressed.

There's more...

We have discussed size optimization of ramdisk built with BusyBox. For the other parts of an embedded Linux system and the other methods, `http://www.elinux.org/System_Size` is a very good reference.

For the kernel parts, we can get more useful information from a project proposed by one of the authors of this book, at `http://elinux.org/Work_on_Tiny_Linux_Kernel`.

Reducing the power consumption of an embedded (Android) system (Advanced)

For most embedded systems, particularly for consumer electronics like smartphone systems, in order to extend battery life and reduce charging time per day, power consumption should be controlled.

The power issue becomes more and more critical in smartphone systems because of the conflicts of higher function requirements and performance requirements, but limited battery capacity and a smaller hardware model.

Getting ready

The whole power-cost optimization topic is very systematic; it is related to hardware system design and the power management policies of the software system.

The hardware elements that need to be considered in the power-cost balance are CPU, memory and external devices, and system components, such as clock, power domain, and regulator.

The corresponding software management topics include CPU idle, CPU frequency, CPU hotplug, memory hotplug, memory frequency, bus frequency, runtime power management, clock management, power domain management, and system suspend.

It's not possible to explain all of them, but we'll introduce an applet that can give us power optimization suggestions, and can measure top power-cost events.

How to do it...

PowerTOP (`https://01.org/powertop/`) is designed to measure, explain, and minimize a computer's electrical power consumption; it not only works on x86 systems, but also supports ARM, AMD, and other kinds of architectures.

1. Enable basic Linux kernel support for PowerTOP:

   To make PowerTOP work, the kernel must be configured with `CONFIG_TIMER_STATS=y`.

   ```
   Kernel hacking   --->
       [*] Collect kernel timers statistics
   ```

   Then compile and flush it to the target platform.

2. Configure PowerTOP in BusyBox:

   BusyBox already has a tiny version of PowerTOP integrated; to use it, make sure it is enabled in the BusyBox configuration.

   ```
   Process Utilities   --->
       [*] powertop
   ```

3. Using PowerTOP:

   Let's run it as follows on the Android emulator:

   ```
   $ adb shell
   shell@android:/ # powertop
   C-state information is not available
   Wakeups-from-idle in 10 seconds: 308
   Top causes for wakeups:
      38.1% (   115)          <interrupt> : Goldfish Timer Tick
      17.9% (    54)         <kernel core> : hrtimer_start (tick_sched_
   timer)
      14.9% (    45)            yaffs-bg-1 : add_timer
   (yaffs_background_waker)
      12.3% (    37)         <kernel core> : hrtimer_start_range_ns
   (tick_sched_timer)
       4.6% (    14)          <interrupt> : goldfish_pipe
       3.6% (    11)     m.android.phone : hrtimer_start_range_ns
   (hrtimer_wakeup)
       3.3% (    10)         <kernel core> : dev_watchdog
   (dev_watchdog)
       3.0% (     9)           VSyncThread : hrtimer_start_range_ns
   ```

```
(hrtimer_wakeup)
    0.7% (    2)        <kernel core> : bdi_arm_supers_timer
(sync_supers_timer_fn)
    0.3% (    1)          <interrupt> : goldfish_fb
    0.3% (    1)    FinalizerWatchd : hrtimer_start_range_ns
(hrtimer_wakeup)
    0.3% (    1)    er.ServerThread : hrtimer_start
(devalarm_hrthandler)
```

We can see that the Goldfish Timer Tick interrupt wakes up the system that is idle for 115 times in 10 seconds. In a real Android device, it may differ from the mentioned outputs.

If the events wake up the system that is idle too frequently, the power cost will be increased remarkably. So, the major causes for wakeups should be attended to and their working frequency should be decreased by tuning the respective kernel drivers.

For example, to reduce the interrupt of Goldfish Timer Tick, the HZ configuration of the Linux kernel should be decreased to reduce the ticks per second; for example, replacing CONFIG_HZ=1000 with CONFIG_HZ=100 may reduce 90 percent system timer interrupts in a second.

How it works...

The ideal working status that is power cost friendly is putting the system into an idle state as far as possible or eventually shutting down all of the devices.

To reduce the power cost of a single device, we should put it into a deeper idle state with less voltage and working frequency (if supported) or power it off eventually if nobody uses it. On the contrary, if some events wake up the device from the idle state to the active state frequently, the device will cost more power; such events are often used as the most important indicators to reduce power cost.

There's more...

We learned about the switching of a system or device state from idle to active and introduced the PowerTOP tool, which can monitor this switching.

In Android, the command dumpsys alarm can track the alarms that wake up the system from a suspend state (a deeper idle state).

But even if we fix all potential wakeup causes, the power cost may still need to be optimized in other aspects. This means even in an idle state, there will be power leaking, which should be fixed up by the GPIO and register settings based on the datasheets of specific chips.

In an active state, power and performance should be balanced carefully with DVFS, clock gating, regulator gating, or power QOS policies.

The system or device should enter into an idle state from an active state timely if there is no activity.

In Android, if there is an activity request, `wake_lock` is held. The system will not switch from an active state to an idle state until the lock is released. To reduce power cost, the lock-holding time should be as short as possible. To track the holding of such wake locks, the `/proc/wakelocks` or `/sys/kernel/debug/wakeup_sources` interface helps, and the `dumpsys power` command may give more related information.

Speeding up the system boot of an embedded (Android) system (Advanced)

For most embedded systems, particularly for consumer electronics like smartphone systems, to reduce the wait time of system power on or start up, the system must be fast enough.

Most embedded devices have strict time limits from power on to showing graphic UI, so speeding the boot time should be considered an important feature.

Getting ready

The following are the basic methods to speed system booting:

  ▸ Disable unused features and functions in all booting components (bootloader, Linux kernel, system, and applications) of an embedded Linux system. This means let the system perform less but necessary jobs.

  ▸ Some initialization procedures can be deferred to the background after the device has booted to a basically workable state.

  ▸ If a multicore CPU is being used, parallize the boot process with multithreads.

  ▸ Based on the considerations of power-cost optimization, set CPU frequency, bus frequency, memory frequency, and even external device working frequency (such as EMMC) as high as possible.

  ▸ Measure the boot procedure and find out the time-cost bottlenecks.

How to do it...

Bootchart (`http://www.bootchart.org/`) is for performance analysis and visualization of the Linux boot process; it can be used for boot speedup optimization.

Android does include the `init` method's built-in `bootchartd` support, but requires the `init` application to be rebuilt; for more details, visit `http://elinux.org/Using_Bootchart_on_Android`.

In our example, we introduce the BusyBox built-in `bootchartd` support to measure the Android system boot procedure.

1. Configure Bootchart in BusyBox:

   First, enable the Bootchart applet in BusyBox.

   ```
   Init Utilities   --->
       [*] bootchartd
       [*]    Compatible, bloated header
       [*]    Support bootchartd.conf
   ```

2. Install BusyBox with `bootchartd` in Android `ramdisk.img`:

   Then, copy the `busybox` binary to Android `ramdisk.img`, create a link `/bootchartd` to `busybox`, and create a `var/log` directory.

   ```
   $ cd ramdisk/
   $ ln -sf busybox /bootchartd
   $ mkdir var/log
   ```

   Recompress the `ramdisk/` to `ramdisk.img` with the following:

   ```
   $ find . | cpio -H newc -o | gzip -9 > ../ramdisk.img
   ```

   The link is for directly using `bootchartd` as the `init` process; the `var/log` directory is for saving the boot log generated by `bootchartd`.

3. Measure the Android system booting with BusyBox `bootchard`:

   Now start the Android emulator.

   ```
   $ emulator @busybox-avd -shell -show-kernel -kernel ./zImage \
       -ramdisk ./ramdisk.img \
       -qemu -append "rdinit=/bootchartd bootchard_init=/init"
   ```

   The `-qemu -append` options allow us to pass extra arguments to the Linux kernel; the preceding `rdinit=/bootchartd` support replaces the default ramdisk `init` with `bootchartd`, and then `bootchartd_init=/init` tells `bootchartd` to start the real `/init` process.

4. Get the bootchartd measuring log:

    After a while, the Android UI will be started and a new file will be created to save the boot logs.

    ```
    shell@android # ls -l /var/log

    total 72

    -rw-r--r--    1 0         0              73334 Jul  5 17:24
    bootlog.tgz
    ```

    Then, pull the logfile into our development system.

    ```
    $ adb pull /var/log/bootlog.tgz
    ```

5. Draw the bootchartd log with pybootchartgui, and analyze it.

    Analyze the boot log with pybootchartgui. This tool can generate a readable graphic output based on the previous boot logfile. In Ubuntu, we can install it simply with the following:

    ```
    $ sudo apt-get install bootchart pybootchartgui
    ```

    Then draw a graph with it.

    ```
    $ bootchart ./bootlog.tgz
    ```

    It may generate an error, such as the header file format is not compatible with the original larger version of the bootchart:

    ```
        File "/usr/lib/pymodules/python2.7/pybootchartgui/draw.py",
    line 341, in draw_header

            txt = headertitle + ': ' +
    mangle(headers.get(headerkey))

            TypeError: cannot concatenate 'str' and 'NoneType'
    objects
    ```

    To work around it, just let the draw.py file of pybootchartgui ignore the errors with except handling.

    ```
    $ vim /usr/lib/pymodules/python2.7/pybootchartgui/draw.py

    338     for (headerkey, headertitle, mangle) in toshow:

    339         header_y += ctx.font_extents()[2]

    340         try:

    341             txt = headertitle + ': ' +
    mangle(headers.get(headerkey))

    342         except:

    343             continue

    344         draw_text(ctx, txt, TEXT_COLOR, off_x, header_y)
    ```

If there are no other issues, we should get results successfully, as shown in the following screenshot:

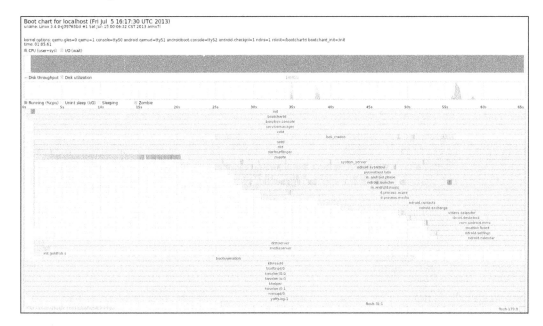

At last, it's time to analyze the graph.

A bootchart picture will have a few of different bits of information that are of interest, especially the CPU and disk load graphs at the top.

There is a timeline running from left to right, with processes shown starting (and sometimes stopping) underneath it. The process CPU loads are indicated by the coloration of its process bar. The things to look for are the start and stop times of the different processes, and their CPU load. Long gaps with low load may mean a timeout or some other issue.

Once you have found out which processes are consuming time during the initialization, we can further check these by looking at the system logs with the logcat tool of Android; running them with strace, a profile (of Android), or perf; and reviewing the corresponding source code.

How it works...

To speed system booting means to reduce the time cost at the system booting stage and also to increase the working frequency of all related devices and meanwhile reduce time cost resources. But, in real practice, the maximal frequency of the devices should be limited to reduce the power cost.

There's more...

The whole booting procedure of an embedded system includes bootloader startup, kernel decompression and bootup, `init` process launching, and system booting. `bootchartd` is mainly for optimization of the booting stage after the `init` process launches.

To measure the boot time of bootloader or the Linux kernel, we can use the Grabserial tool from `http://elinux.org/Grabserial`. For more related resources, visit `http://www.elinux.org/Boot_Time`.

Enhancing the system stability of an embedded (Android) system (Advanced)

For most embedded systems, particularly for consumer electronics like smartphones, due to their complexity, we must apply some policies to strengthen the stability of the system.

Getting ready

System stability is not only for personal computers and server workstations, but is also critically important for embedded systems. Every smartphone user has faced application non-responsiveness, system hangs, and abnormal restart issues; these fall in the scope of system stability. Some common optimization methods include the following:

> ▸ Static checkers and analyzers, such as GCC, Sparse, CocciCheck (`http://coccinelle.lip6.fr/coccicheck.php`), and Smatch (`http://smatch.sourceforge.net/`)
> ▸ Peer to Peer Review; an example of a tool for P2P review is Patchwork (`http://jk.ozlabs.org/projects/patchwork/`)
> ▸ Suitable internal error handling and error tolerance
> ▸ A hardware or software watchdog for external error checks with timeout detection
> ▸ Function testing with enough coverage and batch testing with pressure

How to do it...

Strengthening system stability means fixing the issues mentioned earlier as early as possible and much before the product release stage. System stability is a system feature throughout the development procedure and must be paid more attention.

We'll not discuss all of the methods mentioned previously in detail, but only discuss the part about function testing. To get a stable Linux kernel, we must do a lot of work to test the function of the kernel, device driver, and applications with enough pressure and coverage.

Use the kernel and device drivers as examples; we can test them by writing a set of programs in the shell, and even in the C language. The programs can verify the low-level kernel drivers through the exported `sysfs` and `procfs` or `debugfs` interfaces.

For example, to test the backlight interface of an LCD driver, we write the following piece of shell code:

```
#!/system/bin/sh
# This is a backlight test script
bl_path=/sys/class/backlight/bl_xx/brightness
for i in $(seq 255 -1 1)
do
    sleep 1
    echo $i > $bl_path
done
```

Save it to `bl_test.sh`, and push it to `/system/bin/` in the Android emulator and run it.

```
$ adb remount
$ adb push bl_test.sh /system/bin
$ adb shell chmod 777 /system/bin/bl_test.sh
$ adb shell /system/bin/bl_test.sh
```

Then, we can change the brightness value from 255 to 1 automatically with a 1 second interval. Such scripts can be used to perform basic function verification and pressure testing.

How it works...

System stability in its entirety is a vast topic; it is related to every part of a system, from hardware to software, from the Linux kernel to the Android system and applications.

To improve system stability, the entire project lifecycle must be strictly controlled with standard software QA systems.

Faults should be diagnosed and filtered out during the early requirement analysis, design, and development stages. Delaying them up to the release stage or maintenance stage may cost more resources and even result in financial loss. Errors should be tolerant at runtime.

Test automation is a good method to emulate the using scenes in the release stage. If the test cases are well designed with enough coverage and pressure, most potential issues can be discovered during the testing stage.

There's more...

Here we would like to introduce a project; that is, the Device driver testing framework for TI OMAP. These test cases for OMAP-specific device drivers are written and maintained in an open Git tree. Refer to http://omappedia.org/wiki/OMAP_Kernel_driver_tests. To use this framework for Android, you only need BusyBox and Bash. Both of them have already been introduced before.

We can port this framework to other platforms and develop our own test cases based on this framework; it is good as practice, and left for readers who want to delve into the topic in depth.

For Android applications, CTS and monkeyrunner are available for compatibility and stability testing.

Increasing the serviceability of an embedded (Android) system (Advanced)

At the maintenance stage of a software's lifecycle, techniques to restore the failure generation scene are critical. These include system logging, system debugging, and tracing.

Getting ready

There are some tools available to fix reported failures as quickly as possible.

Android/Linux comes with logging utilities, such as RAM console and Logger/Logcat. They capture data that will allow the conditions associated with the failure to be determined.

The Ftrace-based systrace tool is also added for function-level tracing.

For debugging, gdbserver is available; besides this, the BusyBox top, iostat, and devmem options may give some help. In our example, we will only learn about some of them.

How to do it...

Let's talk about debug filesystems, such as debugfs, sysfs, and procfs and tools, such as Ftrace, top, iostat, and devmem:

1. Kernel debugging interfaces, such as debugfs, sysfs, and procfs:

   To debug the Linux kernel, we should enable its debugging features with CONFIG_DEBUG_KERNEL=y, and further, CONFIG_DEBUG_FS=y creates a virtual debug filesystem (debugfs). We can mount it at runtime.

   ```
   shell@android:/ #  mount -t debugfs none /sys/kernel/debug/
   shell@android:/ #  ls /sys/kernel/debug/
   ```

```
bdi                 hid              mmc0            suspend_stats
wakeup_sources binder              memblock         sched_features
tracing
```

In an Android system, there is a `/d` directory linked to `/sys/kernel/debug/` under the root directory. As we've mentioned before, the Android ramdisk has already mounted `sysfs` and `procfs` to the system. They are useful kernel interfaces, and we can use them to communicate with the kernel, monitor the runtime kernel status, and diagnose issues.

2. Ftrace – tracing kernel functions and events:

   Ftrace is an internal tracing framework in the Linux kernel; it can be used to trace kernel functions. The interface can be found at `/sys/kernel/debug/tracing`. To use it, the following configuration options should be enabled:

```
CONFIG_FTRACE=y
CONFIG_FUNCTION_TRACER=y
CONFIG_FUNCTION_GRAPH_TRACER=y
```

Provided we've configured this and started an emulator with this kernel, we can mount `debugfs` on our Android system, and then enter the tracing directory.

```
shell@android:/ #  cd /sys/kernel/debug/tracing
```

For example, if want to trace kernel functions, we can enable the function tracer.

```
shell@android:/ #  echo function > current_tracer
shell@android:/ #  echo 1 > tracing_on
shell@android:/ #  ls
shell@android:/ #  echo 0 > tracing_on
shell@android:/ #  cat trace | head -20
tracer: function

entries-in-buffer/entries-written: 60151/335518    #P:1
                                _------=> irqs-off
                               / _-----=> need-resched
                              | / _----=> hardirq
/softirq
                              || / _--=> preempt-depth
                              ||| /     delay
           TASK-PID   CPU#   ||||    TIMESTAMP  FUNCTION
              | |        |    ||||       |          |
ActivityManager-328   [000] ....   173.080000: find_pid_ns <-find_
ge_pid
ActivityManager-328   [000] ....   173.080000: pid_nr_ns <-next_
```

```
tgid
ActivityManager-328      [000]  ....    173.080000: pid_task <-next_
tgid
ActivityManager-328      [000]  ....    173.080000: find_ge_pid <-next_
tgid
ActivityManager-328      [000]  ....    173.080000: find_pid_ns <-find_
ge_pid
ActivityManager-328      [000]  ....    173.080000: pid_nr_ns <-next_
tgid
ActivityManager-328      [000]  ....    173.080000: pid_task <-next_
tgid
ActivityManager-328      [000]  ....    173.080000: find_ge_pid <-next_
tgid
ActivityManager-328      [000]  ....    173.080000: find_pid_ns <-find_
ge_pid
```

In reality, Ftrace also provides the other specific tracers, such as the irqsoff and preemptoff tracers. Both of them can be used to find the bottlenecks that may increase system latency. Tracers that are precompiled are listed in the `available_tracers` interface.

```
shell@android:/ # cat /sys/kernel/debug/tracing/available_tracers

blk function_graph mmiotrace wakeup_rt wakeup function nop
```

Besides, it also provides tracepoint- and kprobe-based event tracers that trace some specific group of kernel functions. These groups include a subsystem or a particular kernel module, such as ext4, IRQ, GPIO, power, syscalls, or workqueue. Look at the available events by going to `/sys/kernel/debug/tracing/available_events`. To learn more about Ftrace, read the documents under the `Documentation/trace` directory of the Linux kernel source code.

3. Top – monitors process statuses:

    The `top` applet of BusyBox can be used to monitor processes' status, including CPU and memory utilization. It can display Linux processes, including CPU occupancy, memory usage, and the status of each process. For example:

    ```
    shell@android:/ #  busybox top

    Mem: 253776K used, 511960K free, 0K shrd, 7920K buff, 131144K

    cached

    CPU: 75.7% usr 23.0% sys  1.1% nic  0.0% idle  0.0% io  0.0%
    irq  0.0% sirq

    Load average: 3.92 0.92 0.30 14/245 592

        PID  PPID USER     STAT    VSZ %VSZ CPU %CPU COMMAND
    ```

```
  318     57 1000     S      224m 29.9    0 25.1 system_server
   56      1 1000     S      60308  7.8    0 24.1
/system/bin/surfaceflinger
  377     57 10019    R      162m 21.6    0 14.0 {ndroid.systemui}
com.android.syst
  460     57 10022    S      169m 22.7    0 11.0 {ndroid.launcher}
com.android.laun
  452     57 1001     S      162m 21.6    0  9.1 {m.android.phone}
com.android.phon
  527     57 10009    S      159m 21.2    0  4.1 {d.process.acore}
android.process.
   91      1 1003     S <    23036  3.0    0  3.3 /system/bin/
bootanimation
   59      1 1013     S      21000  2.7    0  2.1 /system/bin/
mediaserver
  382     51 0        R      21072  2.7    0  1.3 /system/bin/fsck_
msdos -p -f /dev/
  559     65 2000     R       1596  0.2    0  0.4 busybox top
   44      2 0        SW         0  0.0    0  0.4 [mmcqd/0]
   57      1 0        S      140m 18.7    0  0.2 zygote /bin/app_
process -Xzygote /
   50      1 1000     S        888  0.1    0  0.2 /system/bin/
servicemanager
    1      0 0        S        348  0.0    0  0.2 /init
  567     57 10009    D      153m 20.4    0  0.0 {ndroid.contacts}
com.android.cont
  505     57 10001    S      151m 20.2    0  0.0 {d.process.media}
android.process.
  439     57 10003    S      151m 20.1    0  0.0 {putmethod.latin}
com.android.inpu
  482     57 10031    S      150m 20.0    0  0.0 {m.android.music}
com.android.musi
   53      1 0        S       9716  1.2    0  0.0 /system/bin/netd
   58      1 1019     S       6612  0.8    0  0.0 /system/bin/
drmserver
```

We can see the verbose outputs. PID shows the process ID, PPID shows the parent process ID of the current process, USER specifies the user ID of each process, STAT represents the status of process, where R is for run and S is for sleep, VSZ shows the virtual memory size used by the process, and %CPU shows the percentage of CPU occupancy of the process.

According to the outputs, we can find which process consumes more system power and system memory and which process is dead, so we can take proper decisions to improve code efficiency and system performance.

4. iostat – monitors the I/O status

    The `iostat` applet of BusyBox is a tool to report CPU and I/O statistics. It will show the average occupation for CPU in idle state; I/O wait response; and the user, system, and steal modes.

    The device status will also be displayed in read/write speed. We can show only CPU stats with the `-c` command and device stats with the `-d` option:

    ```
    shell@android:/d/tracing # busybox iostat -cd
    Linux 3.4.0-g18554c7 (localhost)  07/02/13     _armv71_       (1
    CPU)

    avg-cpu:  %user   %nice %system %iowait  %steal   %idle
              1.30    0.03    1.20    0.00    0.00   97.47
    Device:           tps   Blk_read/s   Blk_wrtn/s   Blk_read
    Blk_wrtn
    mmcblk0          0.22         1.80         0.00      25114
    1
    ```

5. devmem – monitors the hardware status:

    The `devmem` applet of BusyBox is a useful tool to read from or write values to a physical address. This is a very efficient trick to read the hardware register or write an expected value to that register. For example:

    Read the `0x1000000` physical address.

    ```
    shell@android:/ # devmem 0x10000000
    0x00000000
    ```

    Write `0xF000000F` to the `0x10000000` physical address:

    ```
    shell@android:/ # devmem 0x10000000 32 0xF000000F
    shell@android:/ # devmem 0x10000000
    0xF000000F
    ```

    In a real Android device, the **SOC (System On Chip)** has its own CoreSight TM (the ARM debug and trace technology is the most complete on-chip debug and real-time trace solution); it can access from 0 to 4 GB address space, but there are some limits to using these spaces. Some part of this space is used as an **SFR** (Special Function Register) area, and some are used for the physical memory area. So, use `devmem` to see the value of an SFR. We can read its status and change its value if it is writable; this is often used while the system stays in an unstable state.

How it works...

Faults should be filtered out before the maintenance stage, but not all of them can be discovered. If failures occur, logging methods must be provided to record and report the failure scene. With the failure logs, the tracing tools can be used to track the system status and find the problematic areas; lastly, if necessary, use a debugger to debug interactively to locate the problems more precisely.

There's more...

Introduce the Ftrace-based `systrace.py` tool provided by Android.

```
# systrace.py --disk --time=10 -o mynewtrace.html
```

The output `mynewtrace.html` shows the kernel activities graphically and allows us to track the system status easily. The output is in HTML5 format and can be parsed by most modern browsers. For more information about it, visit `http://developer.android.com/tools/help/systrace.html`.

Other similar tools are listed at `http://www.elinux.org/Toolbox`.

We have demonstrated some useful tools provided by BusyBox. With these tools, we can optimize the embedded system for size, stability, power consumption, boot speed, and serviceability. But this is just an initiation for us. We hope you will dig into it further and make more progress in your own embedded system development.

Thank you for buying
Instant Optimizing Embedded Systems Using BusyBox

About Packt Publishing

Packt, pronounced 'packed', published its first book "*Mastering phpMyAdmin for Effective MySQL Management*" in April 2004 and subsequently continued to specialize in publishing highly focused books on specific technologies and solutions.

Our books and publications share the experiences of your fellow IT professionals in adapting and customizing today's systems, applications, and frameworks. Our solution based books give you the knowledge and power to customize the software and technologies you're using to get the job done. Packt books are more specific and less general than the IT books you have seen in the past. Our unique business model allows us to bring you more focused information, giving you more of what you need to know, and less of what you don't.

Packt is a modern, yet unique publishing company, which focuses on producing quality, cutting-edge books for communities of developers, administrators, and newbies alike. For more information, please visit our website: www.packtpub.com.

Writing for Packt

We welcome all inquiries from people who are interested in authoring. Book proposals should be sent to author@packtpub.com. If your book idea is still at an early stage and you would like to discuss it first before writing a formal book proposal, contact us; one of our commissioning editors will get in touch with you.

We're not just looking for published authors; if you have strong technical skills but no writing experience, our experienced editors can help you develop a writing career, or simply get some additional reward for your expertise.

Microsoft Dynamics GP 2013 Cookbook

ISBN: 978-1-84968-938-0 Paperback: 348 pages

Over 110 immediately usable and effective recipes to solve real-world Dynamics GP problems

1. Understand the various tips and tricks to master Dynamics GP, and improve your system's stability in order to enable you to get work done faster

2. Discover how to solve real world problems in Microsoft Dynamics GP 2013 with easy-to-understand and practical recipes

3. Access proven and effective Dynamics GP techniques from authors with vast and rich experience in Dynamics GP

Rapid BeagleBoard Prototyping with MATLAB and Simulink

ISBN: 978-1-84969-604-3 Paperback: 152 pages

Leverage the power of BeagleBoard to develop and deploy practical embedded projects

1. Develop and validate your own embedded audio/video applications rapidly with Beagleboard

2. Create embedded Linux applications on a pure Windows PC

3. Full of illustrations, diagrams, and tips for rapid Beagleboard prototyping with clear, step-by-step instructions and hands-on examples

Please check **www.PacktPub.com** for information on our titles

Instant Buildroot

ISBN: 978-1-78328-945-5   Paperback: 60 pages

Automate the building process of your embedded system and ease the cross-compilation process with Buildroot

1. Learn something new in an Instant! A short, fast, focused guide delivering immediate results

2. Install the Linux kernel configuration and driver along with useful packages such as QT GUI, a web server, and a Telnet remote access server

3. Generate embedded Linux system images

4. Install and configure the U-Boot bootloader

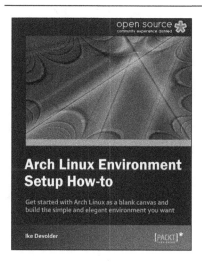

Arch Linux Environment Setup How-to

ISBN: 978-1-84951-972-4   Paperback: 68 pages

Get started with Arch Linux as a blank canvas and build the simple and elegant environment you want

1. Learn something new in an Instant! A short, fast, focused guide delivering immediate results.

2. Install and configure Arch Linux to set up your optimum environment for building applications

3. Boot and manage services, add and remove packages

Please check **www.PacktPub.com** for information on our titles